a cook's bible

seasonal food

HOW TO ENJOY FOOD AT ITS BEST

SUSANNAH BLAKE

DUNCAN BAIRD PUBLISHERS

LONDON

For my father, in memory of his vegetable garden

a cook's bible
seasonal food
Susannah Blake

Distributed in the USA and Canada by Sterling Publishing Co., Inc.
387 Park Avenue South, New York, NY 10016-8810

This edition first published in the UK and USA in 2007 by Duncan Baird Publishers Ltd
Sixth Floor, Castle House, 75-76 Wells Street, London W1T 3QH

Managing Editor: Grace Cheetham
Editor: Cécile Landau
Americanizer: Delora Jones
Managing Designer: Manisha Patel
Studio photography: Diana Miller
Photography assistant: Danielle Wood
Food stylist: Linda Tubby
Food stylist assistant: Rosie Nield
Prop stylist: Róisín Nield
Illustrator: Peter Duggan

Library of Congress Cataloging-in-Publication Data Available

ISBN-13: 978-1-84483-399-3   ISBN-10: 1-84483-399-2

10 9 8 7 6 5 4 3 2 1

Typeset in Interstate and Bergell
Color reproduction by Colourscan, Singapore
Printed in Singapore by Imago

For information about custom editions, special sales, premium and corporate purchases, please
contact Sterling Special Sales Department at 800-805-5489 or specialsales@sterlingpub.com.

Contents

in season

So why do most cooks urge us to try to eat food that is in season? Surely we should rejoice in being able to eat anything we like at any time of the year? Who would not relish fresh strawberries in the depths of winter and asparagus in autumn? Why should we wait until summer to enjoy fresh tomatoes, and what is wrong with eating eggplants in spring? Well, the answer is quite simple—it basically boils down to taste, looking after the environment, and cost.

With very few exceptions, such as medlars, the vast majority of fresh fruits and vegetables have a far superior taste if they are eaten as soon after picking as possible—having been left to to ripen naturally, of course. Although the differences are not too marked for some produce, for others, such as corn and peas, they are huge. A forkful of peas or a bite from an ear of corn, picked a week earlier, packed in plastic, and flown across the world, will leave you with a mouthful of almost tasteless starch. But eat either, plucked fresh from the garden and cooked within minutes, and you will enjoy juicy vegetables, bursting with sweetness and full of flavor.

If flavor is one of your key concerns—which it probably is if you are reading this book—then you should aim to eat locally-grown produce that is in season, so that your food spends as little time as possible between the land and your plate. Eating food that was picked days or weeks ago and has been flown or trucked thousands of miles will never taste as good, no matter how well it is stored and transported. And there are environmental factors to consider, too. With our planet warming up and the polar ice caps melting, should we really be eating food that encourages the excessive burning of fossil fuels simply to get it into our kitchens? It surely makes far more sense to eat food that tastes better, helps to support the local economy, and makes less of a negative impact on our environment.

Cost is another positive reason for eating local produce while it is in season. You should make the most of foods when they are available in abundance. While they are plentiful, they will be far cheaper than when they are scarce or have been flown in from the other side of the world. If you find cherries on the produce shelves at the beginning of spring, they are likely to have a high price tag and will not have the marvelous sweet and tangy flavor of those that have had weeks upon weeks of sunshine to ripen them. So why not wait a couple of months? Then you will able to enjoy a huge and affordable bowl of cherries while they are at their very best. Most of the time, eating seasonally is really just common sense.

NOTES

I am not suggesting, however, that those who live in the northern hemisphere should avoid tropical fruits and vegetables entirely, or that those in cooler climes should never eat an orange again—but that you try to strike a balance by aiming to eat locally and seasonally most of the time. To stop eating imported foods entirely could have a significant impact on the economies of many nations, particularly those in the developing world. Try to stick to imported foods that simply cannot be grown locally and, wherever possible, buy "Fair Trade" certified produce for which the growers have received a fair price. What you choose to eat can have a far-reaching impact on so many people. Thinking just a little more about what you put on your plate can help to improve the quality of life for whole communities.

greater choice

You might assume that aiming to eat whatever is in season from month to month will limit your choice and leave you feeling deprived. But, bizarrely, you may find the exact opposite is true. By trying to buy seasonally, you may end up selecting unfamilar foods and actually introducing greater variety into your diet. Despite the wide choice offered by supermarkets all year round, most people have slowly been reducing the range of foods they eat. With the same fruits and vegetables constantly found on the shelves, we have become less adventurous, sticking to what is familiar and producing a virtually identical shopping list week after week. Tomatoes, zucchinis, lettuces, broccoli, and apples go into the cart regardless, and meals begin to follow a rigid pattern.

By losing our sense of seasonality, we have stopped working with nature's rhythms and have tried to create our own. But often there is no rhythm to what we create. There are no highs and lows, no change, no variety. Many of us seem to have found ourselves with a culinary flatline, in which mealtimes have ceased to be about delicious food at its best and have become just another household chore that requires the minimum of thought and yields the minimum pleasure.

With seasonality, you are forced to make changes, discover new recipes, and actually look forward to an old favorite coming into season. What can be better than gorging yourself on asparagus or apricots in the brief couple of months when they are in season? Overindulge in them, because they will not be around for another nine or ten months. Savor every fruit or vegetable as it comes into its season, then move on and enjoy whatever appears next. Every month, new and wonderful produce will arrive on the shelves—so why not make the most of it while it is plentiful and at its very best?

Compare a tomato reared on little else but water in the depths of winter with a glorious, fat, ruby-red one, ripened naturally in the sun throughout the summer and picked at the beginning of autumn. The difference is marked and unmistakable. Why would you wish to make do with the mushy, tasteless winter tomato, when you could relish the sweet, succulent summer variety just a few months later? And it is not even a question of deprivation. The colder months also offer a whole gamut of tasty produce to enjoy in the meantime, from crinkly savoy cabbages and nutty Brussels sprouts to luscious leeks and hearty root vegetables.

Eating seasonally can bring ingredients that you have never tried before into your life, or remind you of ones that you have forgotten about. One of the great pleasures of writing this book has been rediscovering old favorites of my own, such as Jerusalem artichokes and kale, as well as finding ones that have become a joyous addition to my repertoire. Why, for example, have I been passing by kohlrabi for years? It may look a little odd, but it is delicious and easy to prepare, and I can barely wait for it to be back in season again. Even as I write, I feel a little excited at the prospect of picking up a basketful and taking them home to enjoy as soon as I can.

using the book

The seasons can be fluid and unpredictable. The months in which particular foods arrive can vary according to the weather in any given year as well as from region to region. The sun-soaked Mediterranean will frequently see produce much earlier than, for example, the cooler countries of northern Europe. And in the United States of America and Australia, where there are many different climate zones, ranging from the tropical to the more temperate and even polar conditions, the same produce may enjoy several different seasons within the same country. Also some fruits and vegetables, such as pomegranates, citrus fruits, and avocados, can only be grown in warmer places, while others, such as pears, flourish better in cooler climates.

Not many fruits and vegetables fit neatly into any single season, often arriving in one and fading in another. Some, such as apples, carrots, and beets, keep well and are available from cold-storage long after they have been harvested. So you can still enjoy fresh and locally grown produce, even though it is officially no longer "in season."

NOTES

For the sake of simplicity, the various ingredients covered in this book have been placed in the season or seasons in which they are available in the table on page 219, while they have been divided up according to the season in which they are at their best for the rest of the book. Within the entry for each ingredient, there is detailed information as to when it comes into season and when it is likely to be unavailable. Use this as a basic guide rather than a rigid rule, but, more importantly, stay in touch with what is going on locally, and take into account a hotter or colder growing season than normal, not to mention your own location—whether you live in the tropical South, the Mediterranean-like California, or the frosty North.

As a general rule of thumb, the best way to enjoy fresh, seasonal ingredients is to look out for them in your local farmers' market or farm shop. If you always try to buy fresh, locally-grown produce—by default, it should be in season. If you are at a vegetable stand and the place of origin is not marked, ask where it was grown. A good grocer will be happy to help and, if you show interest, will always be pleased to point out what is best on the shelves at any particular time. Home-delivery of farm-fresh produce are a good idea, too—if you don't know of one in your area, check the Internet. Some farms may also offer pick-your-own boxes, so you will know exactly how long your food has taken to get from the ground to your plate.

And of course, for avid gardeners, growing your own is a fabulous way to enjoy truly fresh food. But a word of warning—there is a potential downside to this type of enterprise, too. If you are champing at the bit to get going on your own seasonal vegetable patch, do spend a little time planning your planting and harvesting carefully to ensure you can enjoy a reasonable variety of food, and avoid gluts of produce all arriving at the same time. When I was a child, my father was a keen gardener with his own garden plot, which meant I had a wonderfully varied diet, far, far richer than that of most of my school friends. After all, who else got to enjoy a plateful of asparagus every night in late spring and early summer, just hours after it had been picked? However, when a bowl brimming with fresh raspberries was presented for the 40th time one summer, I began to lose my relish. After the raspberry glut of 1979, I was almost into adulthood before I was able to really enjoy a dish of those glorious fruits again. So you actually *can* have too much of a good thing!

cooking and its natural rhythms

Throughout time, cuisines have developed around the world founded on the seasons, combining ingredients that are available at the same time to make dishes which suit the weather. And as each new ingredient was introduced from faraway lands and cultivated in its new home, so it would be assimilated into the cuisine. From such a history comes a wonderful heritage of recipes that we can still enjoy and use to help take advantage of today's seasonal produce.

It is no coincidence that throughout the world the same ingredients are frequently found together in recipes. Fresh mint, for example, is a common flavoring for both peas and lamb. The herb enhances the taste of both, but part of the reason that such a combination is so popular is that the ingredients involved come into season at a similar time. In Morocco, Italy, and Greece, you will find numerous classic dishes in which artichokes and peas are braised or stewed together, with new potatoes being another regular addition—an obvious mix, when you think of how their seasons overlap. In France, they like to braise lettuces and peas together, with a hint of zesty mint—the perfect light accompaniment on a hot summer day. From Greece and Turkey, through the Middle East and into India, cucumber, yogurt, and mint are another classic blend, whether it is in *tzatziki*, *cacik*, *raita*, or one of the other numerous similar dishes. Cucumbers and mint are available in abundance at the same time and bring out the best in each other.

Look at the foods we enjoy in spring. After a harsh winter of sturdy, strongly flavored brassicas, starchy root vegetables, and warming stews and roasts, the days grow longer and temperatures rise, and with them the shoots and leaves of the new year. So it makes sense that these tender, delicately flavored morsels should now be savored. Freshly picked asparagus is cooked until tender to enjoy with just a little melted butter or hollandaise sauce. Artichokes are unwrapped leaf by leaf, as the succulent flesh is sucked off each one, until you reach the creamy heart. Surely it is no coincidence that we make such a sensuous drama of enjoying these fresh new pickings after a season of cold and austerity? Think of all the tender spring greens that provide light salads, perked up with punchy scallions and fresh herbs, or the excitement of tart, pink rhubarb for turning into pies and fools (a whipped cream dish) and crumble—a refreshing addition to the dessert menu after the apples and pears and dried fruits of winter.

NOTES

It is not just the ingredients that have their natural rhythms, but our approach to them works with the seasons, too. Spring is the time to relish the arrival of all things new, and marks a move away from the sustaining, warming, and comforting dishes that feel so necessary in winter. In contrast, summer makes the most of all those sweet and juicy, crisp and tender, sun-ripened fruits and vegetables—with lighter dishes, including wonderful chilled soups and desserts, to suit the hot weather. And summer dishes make the most of the seasonal abundance that generally accompanies a rise in temperature. Those Mediterranean classics that thrive in the warm sunshine are teamed together: tomatoes, zucchinis, eggplants, and red bell peppers sit side-by-side again and again in salads and stews: from French *ratatouille* and Turkish *turlu turlu* to the Middle Eastern salad *fattoush* and Italian *panzanella*. In autumn, dishes warm up again—not only in temperature but in their flavors and textures, too—sweet, meltingly soft roast squashes, plum tarts, game cooked with autumn fruits and luscious, earthy wild mushrooms. Dishes are served up that make the most of the rich harvest that was slowly moving towards maturity during the the long, sultry days of summer.

Until recently, what people ate has always been guided by the seasons. It is only lately that summer blueberries have been paired with autumn and winter game, that asparagus has been appearing on Thanksgiving and Christmas canapés, and that rhubarb and raspberries have become a classic partnership. Of course, this has only become possible with the effectiveness of freezing certain fruits, vegetables and herbs, and it may be no bad thing when the produce has been frozen at its peak. With summer produce such as tomatoes, this kind of approach can make sense—but for the main why not heed the common sense of eating food at its peak and draw on years of experience by making the most of truly seasonal ingredients?

I am not suggesting for a moment that we should cook and eat only the foods our parents and grandparents did. Cooking offers a wonderful opportunity for constantly developing new flavors, for reworking and experimenting, for allowing one dish to evolve into another—but if the original foundations are solid, why try to replace them with something less firm and secure? A good common-sense approach to successful cooking is to ensure that the basic ingredients of a dish are good; using mediocre ingredients makes it much harder to turn out something fabulous. Make the most of what you have, relish ingredients when they are at their best, draw on the experience of millions of cooks down the centuries and it will be quite difficult to go wrong. But most of all enjoy food for what it is—something natural and delicious.

the seasonal pantry

Throughout the culinary year, you will find yourself relying more or less on staples from the pantry or cupboard, according to what is in season. For example, in autumn and winter, when you are cooking more substantial dishes, you may find yourself using more dried grains, legumes, and pasta, and relying more on dried fruit, while there is less fresh produce available. Canned tomatoes, for example, are perfect for winter stews and soups and are a vast improvement on the tasteless, unseasonal fresh ones that you will find in the supermarkets at that time.

However, whatever the weather and whatever the season, it is always a good idea to keep well-stocked cupboards, containing all the basics. You can add to this list with your own, or store-bought, preserved ingredients that have been pickled, canned, frozen, or dried while the fresh ingredients were in abundance and at their best.

staples

Ingredients such as rice, pasta, and beans can provide the foundation of many meals—whether a summer salad, hearty winter stew, or warming autumnal risotto. It is worth keeping a bag of long-grain rice (quick-cook, basmati, white, or brown), as well as one of creamy risotto rice, in the cupboard. With pasta, make sure you have a package of nodles such as spaghetti or linguine, and a package of pasta shapes, such as penne (mostaccioli) or fusilli (spirals). Beans and legumes are another useful standby. Keep some canned as well as dried ones, as the canned beans can save time on soaking and boiling. Other useful staples include couscous, bulgur, lentils, flour (all-purpose, self-rising, and bread flour, if you're inclined to make your own bread), raising agents such as baking soda and powder, and sugar (brown, white, and confectioners').

oils and vinegars

Every cook should have in the cupboard a bottle of olive oil and a bottle of sunflower or vegetable oil – essential for sautéeing, frying, roasting, and dressings. Aim also to have a bottle each of balsamic vinegar, white wine vinegar, and red wine vinegar. You can flavor oils and vinegars by adding sprigs of herbs such as tarragon, thyme, or rosemary, or spices such as coriander seed or chili.

NOTES

spices, herbs, and other flavorings

Although many spices can be grown only in warmer climates, they are an essential in any kitchen. Most are dried and have a long shelflife, so it is worth investing in a good variety. Basics include cumin, coriander seed, chili, paprika, turmeric, cardamom, ginger, cinnamon, nutmeg, and peppercorns. Store them in a cool, dark place and remember that whole spices retain their flavor longer than ground ones. Dried herbs are a useful standby, but many do not retain their flavor well. Frozen herbs offer a more authentic flavor out of season—particularly the more delicate, tender herbs such as basil, parsley, and cilantro—so, if you can, freeze your own while they are in season. Other useful flavorings include mustards (Dijon and whole-grain) and sauces such as soy sauce, sweet chili sauce, fish sauce, and Tabasco sauce.

fresh herbs

Fresh herbs are not strictly a cupboard ingredient, but to enjoy them at the peak of their flavor it is well worth trying to grow your own if you can—whether it is in a tub on a rooftop terrace, in a corner of the garden, or on a sunny windowsill. Generally, this requires little skill and, apart from the superior flavor that homegrown herbs bring to dishes, using them is so much cheaper than buying a bunch of fresh ones every time you need them. Hardier herbs, such as rosemary, thyme, chives, sage, and mint, are very easy to grow, although the more delicate varieties, such as basil, cilantro (coriander leaves), and tarragon can prove more difficult, so you may prefer to buy these as and when you need them. Alternatively you can buy them already growing in a pot, and if you keep them on a sunny windowsill, they should thrive.

preserving seasonal ingredients

One of the best ways to enjoy seasonal ingredients throughout the year is by preserving them while they are abundant and at their best, by making them into jams, jellies, pickles, or chutneys.

STERILIZING, SEALING, AND LABELING PRESERVES: When making jams, jellies, and other preserves, it is essential to sterilize your jars before you fill them and then to seal them properly. They should then be left until the contents have cooled, when a label should be attached, stating clearly what each jar contains, along with the date.

There are various ways to sterilize jars and lids. The easiest is to use a dishwasher. Put the jars and lids in the dishwasher and run it on its hottest setting. Alternatively, put the jars and lids in a large pot and pour hot water in and around them to cover. Bring to a boil and boil for 10 minutes, then remove and drain upside-down.

Different preserves can be sealed in different ways. After canning, sweet jams and jellies can be covered with a wax-paper disc, then the neck of the jar sealed with cellophane, held in position with an elastic band, or sealed with a screwtop lid. Acidic chutneys and relishes should be sealed with non-metallic lids (as the vinegar in them corrodes metal). Canned fruits and pickled vegetables can be sealed in clamp-top jars with rubber seals.

MAKING JELLIES: Clear, sparkling jellies are made by boiling fruit with water, then straining the juice through a jelly bag or cheesecloth and then boiling it with sugar (usually 1 pound sugar [about 2½ cups] to every 2½ cups juice) to a temperature of 220°F. Depending on the fruit, the jellies may be served as an accompaniment to roast meats or as a sweet preserve on buttered toast, on scones spread with cream cheese, or in a peanut butter and jelly sandwich.

To make red currant jelly (this method can also be used as a guide for other fruits), strip 2 pounds (about 8 cups) red currants from their stalks and place in a heavy pan with ¾ cups water. Bring to a boil and simmer gently for about 30 minutes, stirring occasionally, until the fruit is very soft. Gently squash the fruit with the back of the spoon, then pour the fruit and juices into a sterilized jelly bag suspended over a large bowl and let it drain until juice stops dripping from the bag. (Do not squeeze the bag to speed the process, as this will result in a cloudy jelly.) Measure the juice collected in the bowl, pour into a clean pan, and add 1 pound (about 2½ cups) sugar for every 2½ cups juice. Heat gently, stirring until the sugar dissolves, then bring to a boil and boil rapidly to a temperature of 220°F. Remove from the heat, skim off any scum, pour into sterilized jars, and seal. Let them cool, label clearly, and store in a cool, dark place.

MAKING JAMS: Softly-set jams and sweet fruit preserves are delicious spread on bread, toast, scones, and muffins, and in between layer cakes. They are particularly good made with soft summer fruits, such as berries, cherries, currants, apricots, and peaches. They are usually made with similar amounts of fruit and sugar. You may need to add a little water or fruit juice to the less juicy fruits such as peaches and apricots.

NOTES

To make raspberry jam (this method can also be used as a basic technique for other fruits, although you will need to add an extra teaspoon of lemon juice when using low-pectin fruits, such as strawberries and cherries), put 1 pound raspberries (about 3 cups) and 1 teaspoon lemon juice in a large pot, place over a low heat, until the juices begin to run, then let it simmer gently for about 10 minutes. Crush the fruit with the back of a spoon and add 1 pound (about 2½ cups) sugar. Stir over a low heat until the sugar has dissolved, then bring to a boil and boil rapidly, stirring occasionally, until the temperature reaches 220°F. Remove from the heat and skim off any scum. Pour into sterilized jars and seal. Let cool completely, label and date the jars clearly, and store in a cool, dark place.

BOTTLING FRUITS: Preserving fruits in alcohol is a quick, simple, and delicious way to enjoy them throughout the year, long after their season has ended. Fruit that has been treated in this way is excellent served with ice cream and other creamy desserts, such as panna cotta and cheesecake, and the richly flavored liqueur can be strained and enjoyed on its own.

The recipe that follows for bottling soft summer fruits is based on the classic German preserve *rumtopf*, in which different fruits would be added to the jar as and when they came into season. Prepare 2 pounds summer fruits, such as strawberries, cherries, blueberries, raspberries, black currants, and red currants, by hulling, pitting, and removing the stalks as necessary, and cutting any larger fruits into bite-size pieces. Put all the fruit into a large bowl, sprinkle 1¼ cups sugar over them, cover and let stand for about 1 hour. Spoon the fruit, along with any juices that have formed, into a sterilized canning jar and pour about 4 cups rum over the top to cover. Cover the top of the jar with plastic wrap, then seal and store in a cool dark place for about 2 months before serving.

MAKING PICKLES, CHUTNEYS, AND RELISHES: Preserved with salt and vinegar, these are good for serving with cold meats and cheeses and in sandwiches. Chutneys and relishes have a more jam-like consistency, while the ingredients used in pickles are usually left whole or cut in half, and are preserved in a flavored vinegar. Once pickles, chutneys, or relishes have been opened, they should be stored in the fridge.

The recipe that follows is for a fruity peach chutney, but a similar technique can be used for other fruits and vegetables, such as mangoes and tomatoes. Put 2 cups red wine vinegar in a large pot with 1½ cups light brown sugar, 1 cup golden raisins, 1 teaspoon ground cinnamon, and 1 teaspoon ground allspice, and heat gently, stirring, until the sugar dissolves. Bring to a boil, then add 1 pound (about 3-4 medium) peaches, that have been peeled, pitted, and roughly chopped, 3 sliced onions, 2 green chilies that have been seeded and chopped, 3 crushed cloves garlic, 2 teaspoons freshly grated ginger root, and 1 teaspoon salt. Return to a boil, then reduce the heat and let simmer, stirring frequently, for about 45 minutes until the chutney is thick. Spoon into warmed sterilized jars, seal, and let cool before labeling. Keep in a cool place for at least 2 weeks before serving.

drying seasonal ingredients

Many seasonal ingredients can be successfully dried so that you can enjoy them at a later date. Drying may alter the flavor of some foods, but not necessarily in a bad way. Ingredients that are particularly well suited to drying include mushrooms, chilies, and herbs.

DRYING MUSHROOMS: Many wild mushrooms such as cèpes (porcini), chanterelles, and morels can be dried, then rehydrated by soaking in warm water for about 30 minutes before cooking. Drying tends to intensify the taste of mushrooms and a few added to a risotto or stew made with cultivated mushrooms can give the flavor a real boost.

The simplest way to dry most mushrooms is to slice them, arrange them on a tray in a single layer, and then leave them a warm place for several days until dry. They should be stored in an airtight container until ready to use.

DRYING CHILIES: Use dried chilies whole, crumbled into dishes, or rehydrated before use. Drying is an excellent way to preserve fresh chilies if you grow your own. Simply spread them out on a tray in a single layer and leave in a warm place for several days to dry. Store in an airtight container until ready to use.

DRYING FRESH HERBS: Although freezing fresh herbs retains much more of their flavor, drying is also a good way of preserving them for later use. Home-dried herbs usually have a better flavor than commercially dried ones. Spread the leaves out on a tray in a single layer and leave in a warm place for several days until dry. Store in an airtight container until ready to use.

freezing seasonal ingredients

The invention of the freezer has been a boon for the keen cook. Many fresh ingredients freeze incredibly well, so they can be enjoyed later in the year when they are no longer in season. Ingredients that are particularly worth freezing include fresh herbs, soft summer fruits, and vegetables such as corn and peas that deteriorate in flavor rapidly after picking. It is also worth cooking certain ingredients while they are readily available and cheap, as well as preparing and freezing certain dishes for later use. Make use of the abundance of sweet, juicy tomatoes in summer by preparing a huge pot of fresh tomato sauce and freezing it for use in recipes during the cooler months of the year. Poached fruits such as plums and apricots also freeze well and can make a wonderful treat in winter, when the choice of fresh fruit is limited.

FREEZING SUMMER FRUITS: Soft summer berries and currants freeze well and can be the focus of wonderful desserts in autumn and winter, when they are no longer in season. Freezing, however, will affect their texture, so they are best used in desserts such as crumbles or pies or as a topping on a cheesecake, in which the fruit is cooked. To freeze these fruits, prepare them by hulling and stripping off stems as necessary, then spread them out on a baking sheet lined with waxed paper. Freeze, then transfer to freezer bags or containers for long-term storage.

FREEZING HERBS: Freezing is a great way to preserve the delicious flavor of fresh herbs, particularly delicate ones such as cilantro (coriander leaves) and basil. Frozen herbs, however, are not really suitable for garnishing and are best used for stirring into cooked dishes. There are numerous methods of freezing herbs, but the simplest one is to chop the herbs, then place them in an airtight container in the freezer. They freeze in a loose mass, so you can remove a teaspoonful or so at a time, as and when you need them.

NOTES

Spring

From tender stems of asparagus and the first crunchy carrots of the year to earthy new potatoes and (in England) glorious purple sprouting broccoli, spring marks the end of the winter chill, a move towards warmth and sunshine and the sprouting of all things new. Spiky artichokes, crisp scallions, long pink sticks of tangy rhubarb, fragrant spring herbs, and a wonderful array of succulent young greens—from sorrel and dandelion leaves to peppery arugula and the first lettuces of the year—all provide a welcome change after the sturdy cabbages, leeks, and cauliflowers of winter. With the new season's lamb comes an exciting array of sheep's milk cheeses, with their creamy texture and distinctive tart flavor. Many wild mushrooms may now be out of season, but the delicious morel, with its eye-catching honeycombed cap, provides a real gourmet treat. Its delicious smoky taste marks it out as ideal for sautéeing in butter or cooking with a creamy sauce and serving on polenta wedges—a wonderful base for their intense flavor.

spring herbs

After the robustly flavored herbs of autumn, such as rosemary and sage, and the dried herbs of winter, the arrival of an abundance of fresh, tender, aromatic herbs in spring marks a whole new turn in the culinary calendar. Long, thin, oniony chives are wonderful chopped and sprinkled onto salads, into omelets, and stirred into risottos. They add a freshness that cooked onions can barely touch upon, along with a vibrant splash of color. Aromatic dill, with its unmistakeable anise flavor, is delicious paired with cream and eggs, and is particularly good with fish. Sharp, zesty mint adds an uplifting tang to countless dishes, both sweet and savory. Try it tossed into salads, dressings, and desserts, or sprinkled over Middle Eastern and Asian dishes. Mint really is one of the most versatile of the spring herbs and its powerful fragrance seems to mirror all that is fresh and new about the season. Then there is plenty of parsley too, and marjoram and oregano, both adding the distinct aromas that are so redolent of the Mediterranean kitchen.

Marinated chicken with tabbouleh

SERVES 4
4 skinless chicken breasts
1 clove garlic, crushed
juice of 1 lemon
¼ tsp. dried red pepper flakes
1 tbsp. olive oil

FOR THE TABBOULEH
⅔ cup bulgur
salt and freshly ground black pepper
1 handful fresh mint leaves, chopped
2 oz. fresh flat-leaf parsley, chopped (about 1 cup)
2 tomatoes, peeled, seeded, and chopped
2 tbsp. olive oil
juice of 1 lemon

Arrange the chicken in a single layer in a shallow dish. Whisk together the garlic, lemon juice, red pepper flakes, and olive oil, then season with salt and pour it over the chicken breasts, turning them to coat well. Cover and leave in the fridge to marinate for at least 1 hour.

Heat the oven to 425°F. Put the bulgur in a bowl, add a pinch of salt, and pour enough boiling water over it to cover. Let it soak for 20 minutes until tender. Drain well, then set aside.

Put the chicken breasts on a baking sheet, pour the marinade over them, and bake in the oven for 20 minutes, until cooked.

Meanwhile, toss together the drained bulgur with the chopped herbs and tomatoes in a large bowl. Drizzle the olive oil and lemon juice over them and season to taste with salt and pepper. Serve with the hot chicken.

NOTES

Risotto with spinach and spring herbs

This addictive risotto is a combination of some of the best spring has to offer—a creamy blend of rice and tender young spinach greens, infused with aromatic dill and chives.

SERVES 4

4¾ cups vegetable stock
2 tbsp. butter
1 onion, finely chopped
2 cloves garlic, finely chopped
1½ cups risotto rice
¾ cup white wine
9 oz. baby spinach leaves (about 4-5 large handfuls)
1 cup grated Parmesan cheese, plus extra for sprinkling
handful of fresh dill, chopped
¼ cup chopped fresh chives
salt and freshly ground black pepper

Pour the stock into a saucepan and bring to a boil. Reduce the heat and keep at a very low simmer.

Melt the butter in another large pan. Add the onion and garlic and cook gently over medium heat for about 5 minutes, until soft. Add the risotto rice and cook, stirring, for another 2 minutes.

Pour in the wine and simmer, stirring continuously, until all the liquid has been absorbed. Add a ladleful of the hot stock and continue to simmer, stirring, until the stock has been absorbed. Continue cooking in this way for about 18-20 minutes, until the rice is almost tender and most of the stock has been used up.

Stir in the spinach and cook for another minute or so until the greens are tender and wilted. Remove the pan from the heat, stir in the grated Parmesan and chopped dill and chives, and season to taste with salt and pepper. Serve immediately, with extra Parmesan sprinkled on top.

Herb salad with sheep's milk cheese

SERVES 4

1½ tbsp. cider vinegar
3 tbsp. olive oil
½ tsp. sugar
2 tsp. finely chopped fresh mint
salt and freshly ground black pepper
3 large handfuls of spring salad greens, such as arugula, lollo rosso lettuce, and baby beet greens
large handful of fresh herbs, such as cilantro, parsley, sorrel, and chives
2 apples
4 oz. sheep's milk cheese, such as Romano or Manchego, shaved into thin slices (about 1½ -2 cups)

Whisk together the cider vinegar, olive oil, sugar, and mint in a small bowl to make a dressing. Season to taste with salt and pepper and set to one side.

Put the salad greens and herbs in a large serving bowl and toss together to combine.

Core the apples and cut into wedges. Scatter these, along with the cheese shavings, over the salad greens and herbs. Drizzle with the prepared dressing and toss to mix well.

Serve immediately.

Lamb skewers with mint salsa (opposite)

SERVES 4

18 oz. lean lamb, trimmed and cut
into 1-inch cubes
(about 2¼ cups)
2 cloves garlic, crushed
2 tsp. ground cumin
2 tbsp. red wine vinegar
1 tbsp. olive oil
salt and freshly ground black pepper

FOR THE MINT SALSA

1 English cucumber, peeled, seeded,
and chopped
1 tomato, peeled, seeded, and
chopped
3 tbsp. chopped fresh mint leaves
handful of fresh flat-leaf parsley,
chopped
3 scallions, thinly sliced
¼ tsp. sugar
1 tsp. white wine vinegar
1 tbsp. olive oil

Put the cubes of lamb into a large bowl. Whisk together the garlic, cumin, vinegar, and olive oil in a small bowl, then season to taste with salt and pepper. Pour this mixture over the lamb, toss to coat, then cover and let marinate in the fridge for at least 2 hours.

To make the salsa, mix together the cucumber, tomato, chopped mint and parsley, and scallions in a serving bowl. In a separate bowl, stir the sugar into the vinegar until it has dissolved, then whisk in the olive oil and season to taste with salt and pepper. Pour this over the cucumber, tomato, and herb mixture and toss to combine. Check the seasoning and add more salt or pepper if necessary. Set aside and keep cool until ready to use.

Heat the broiler to hot. Remove the lamb from the fridge and thread the cubes of meat onto 8 skewers. Place under the broiler for 8-10 minutes, turning halfway through the cooking time, until well browned and cooked to your liking. Serve with the salsa.

Broiled salmon with lemon and dill sauce

Tangy and brimming with the fragrance of fresh dill, the simple creamy sauce, served here with salmon, will make a good match for any type of broiled or baked fish.

SERVES 4

4 salmon fillets or steaks, around
7 oz. each
salt and freshly ground black pepper
6 tbsp. mayonnaise
1½ tsp. Dijon mustard
3 tbsp. lemon juice
1½ tsp. grated lemon rind
4 tbsp. finely chopped fresh dill
pinch of sugar

Heat the broiler to hot. Season the salmon with salt and pepper, then place under the broiler for about 6 minutes, turning halfway through the cooking time, until just cooked through.

While the fish is broiling, put the mayonnaise, mustard, and lemon juice and rind into a bowl and whisk together until smooth and creamy. Stir in the dill, then add the sugar and season to taste with salt and pepper. Serve this sauce with the freshly broiled fish.

spring greens

Tender young leaves, sprouting from the earth along with the other spring shoots, are a refreshing seasonal treat after the hardier greens of winter. The first lettuces—the succulent round variety and the sweet Bibbs and romaines—arrive, making a perfect base for a host of light, healthy salads. They are delicious combined with the freshly unfurled leaves of other spring plants, such as spinach, arugula, watercress, beet greens, and even wild nettles and dandelions, creating a delightful mix of colors and flavors. The torn leaves of tangy lemony sorrel also make a wonderful zesty addition to the salad bowl and can give an extra lift to soups and sauces, especially those to go with fish and poultry. And there are hardier spring greens, too, such as collard greens. A close relation to kale, their dark green leaves are picked before a heart forms, or may be grown as a special non-heart-forming variety. They can be cooked and served in the same way as curly winter kale and they make a delicious accompaniment to roast spring lamb.

Smoked mackerel fishcakes with sorrel sauce

SERVES 4

1 lb. smoked mackerel fillets
1 lb. potatoes (about 4 medium), boiled
2 scallions, trimmed and finely chopped
salt and freshly ground black pepper
2 tbsp. flour
1 egg, beaten
about 3-4 cups dried bread crumbs
oil, for frying

FOR THE SORREL SAUCE

½ cup white wine
½ cup heavy cream
large handful of sorrel (about 3½ oz.), finely shredded

Remove the skin from the mackerel and flake the flesh into a large bowl. Mash the potatoes, then add to the mackerel along with the scallions, and stir to mix. Season with black pepper, then shape the mixture into 8 round patties.

Heap the flour onto a plate. Dip each patty into the flour to coat, then dip in the egg and roll in the bread crumbs until well covered. Place in the fridge to chill for about 20 minutes.

Meanwhile make the sauce. Put the wine and cream in a pan and heat to a gentle simmer. Stir in the sorrel until just wilted. Season to taste with salt and pepper and set aside and keep warm while cooking the fishcakes.

Heat the oil in a frying pan. Add the prepared fishcakes and fry for about 3 minutes on each side, until crisp and golden. Drain on paper towels and serve with the sauce poured over them.

NOTES

Chilled spring-greens soup

Sorrel gives this soup a lovely lemony tang, while arugula lends it a peppery bite. You can use other spring greens such as nettles in place of some of the arugula and spinach, but keep the quantity of sorrel the same because it really does add an essential zing.

SERVES 4
8 oz. potatoes, cut up
4 cups vegetable stock
2 bunches scallions, trimmed and sliced
3 large handfuls spinach, roughly shredded
1 large handful arugula, roughly shredded
1½ large handfuls sorrel, roughly shredded
scant cup white wine
½ cup heavy cream
salt and freshly ground black pepper

Put the potatoes and stock in a large pot, bring to a boil, then reduce the heat, cover, and simmer for about 10 minutes until the potatoes are tender.

Add the scallions, spinach, arugula, and sorrel, then cover and simmer for about 2 minutes until the greens are wilted.

Pour the soup into a food processor or blender and blend to a smooth puree. Stir in the wine and cream. Season to taste with salt and pepper, let cool, then place in the fridge to chill for at least 2 hours before serving.

Linguine with arugula pesto

Peppery arugula makes a great alternative to basil in this fresh green pesto. You can substitute the pine nuts for other nuts such as hazelnuts or almonds if you like.

SERVES 4
11 oz. linguine
salt and freshly ground black pepper
⅓ cup pine nuts
1 clove garlic, chopped
2 large handfuls of arugula
¼ cup olive oil
1 cup grated Parmesan cheese, plus extra for serving

Cook the linguine in a large pot of boiling salted water according to the instructions on the package. Drain well, reserving about 4 tablespoons of the cooking water.

Meanwhile, prepare the pesto. Put the pine nuts, garlic, arugula, and olive oil in a food processor and blend until smooth, then stir in the grated Parmesan cheese.

Add the pesto and 3-4 tablespoons of the reserved cooking water to the freshly cooked pasta. Toss well to combine, then season with plenty of black pepper. Serve immediately, sprinkled with more grated Parmesan cheese.

NOTES

Spring

Mixed-greens salad with seared beef and garlic dressing

The peppery bite of wasabi, a relation of horseradish, gives this fresh, fruity spring salad a real kick—perfect with tender, juicy, seared beef.

SERVES 4

9 oz. piece sirloin beef
4 tbsp. olive oil
1 clove garlic, crushed
1 tsp. wasabi paste
1 tbsp. cider vinegar
pinch of sugar
2 tsp. finely chopped fresh mint leaves
salt
2 large handfuls mixed spring greens, such as arugula, baby spinach, and nettles
2 pears, peeled, cored, and cut into thin wedges
handful of hazelnuts, toasted and chopped

Trim off any fat or sinew from the meat and brush with about ½ tablespoon of the oil. Heat a grill pan or broiler until very hot, brush the pan with a little more of the oil, then press the meat down on it for about 2 minutes. Flip it over and cook for 2 more minutes, then cook for another 2 minutes on each side, or until cooked to your taste. Lift the meat onto a board, cover with foil, and let rest for 10 minutes.

Meanwhile, whisk together the garlic, wasabi, vinegar, sugar, and remaining oil. Stir in the mint and season to taste with salt. Set aside.

Arrange the greens on four serving plates and scatter the pear wedges and hazelnuts over the top. Slice the beef thinly and scatter it over the salad, then drizzle with the dressing and serve.

Spring greens with lemon and garlic

Buy only loosely packed heads of spring greens that are crisp and deep green with no signs of yellowing. As with other members of the cabbage family, they should be cooked until just tender, retaining some bite—avoid overcooking at all costs.

SERVES 4

2 heads of spring greens, finely shredded
salt and freshly ground black pepper
2 tbsp. olive oil
2 cloves garlic, finely chopped
juice of 1 lemon

Plunge the shredded greens into a large pot of boiling salted water for 2-3 minutes until just tender. Drain well.

Meanwhile, heat the oil in a large frying pan, add the garlic, and gently fry for about 1 minute. Toss in the drained greens and season to taste with salt and pepper. Stir in the lemon juice and serve immediately.

spinach

Although it is available for most of the year, spinach is one of the highlights of spring. Then its tender young greens make such a refreshing change after the sturdy greens and hearty roots of winter. First cultivated in Persia, but now a staple of cuisines worldwide, spinach is a versatile vegetable. The soft baby leaves can be used raw in salads or make a lovely addition to risottos, stir-fries, and even mashed potato; larger leaves, sautéed with a little garlic, then seasoned and served with a squeeze of lemon, make a delicious accompaniment to broiled meats and fish.

Spinach has a natural affinity with butter, cheese, cream, and eggs, but is also delicious matched with various herbs and spices. In India, a blend of spiced spinach and potato is often served with rice or flatbreads. In Spain, it is cooked with garlic, raisins, and pine nuts to make a popular tapas dish, while in the Middle East it is added to stews and used in fillings for pies and pastries.

Choose fresh-looking leaves, and avoid any that are yellowing, wilting, or becoming slimy. Cut off tough stems and always wash well in cold water to remove any soil or grit. Then shake off as much water as possible, patting the leaves dry on paper towels if necessary, before cooking in a dry, tightly covered pan for a few minutes, until they have wilted. Spinach gives off a lot of liquid while cooking, so always drain well before serving or using in a recipe.

Baby spinach and new potato salad with melting Gorgonzola (opposite)

SERVES 4
1 lb., 5 oz. new potatoes
salt and freshly ground black pepper
1 tbsp. balsamic vinegar
2 tbsp. olive oil
½ tsp. whole-grain mustard
2 large handfuls baby spinach
6 oz. Gorgonzola cheese, cut into bite-size pieces (about 1½ cups)

If the potatoes are on the large side, cut into bite-size pieces. Add to a pot of boiling salted water and cook for about 10 minutes until tender. Drain well.

Meanwhile, prepare a dressing by whisking together the vinegar, olive oil, and mustard in a small bowl. Season to taste with salt and pepper, then set aside.

Arrange the spinach leaves on four serving plates and scatter the Gorgonzola cheese over the top, followed by the hot potatoes. Drizzle the dressing over them, toss to combine, and serve immediately.

NOTES

Spanakopita

SERVES 6

2 tbsp. olive oil
1 onion, finely chopped
18 oz. spinach
3 large eggs
7 oz. feta cheese, drained
and crumbled (about 1¾ cups)
handful of fresh dill,
roughly chopped
freshly ground black pepper
5 oz. phyllo pastry dough sheets
3 tbsp. butter, melted

Heat the oven to 375°F. Grease an 8 x 10-in. baking dish.

Heat the oil in a large pot. Add the onion and gently fry for about 5 minutes, until soft. Meanwhile, wash the spinach well and shake off as much water as possible. Stir the spinach into the onion, cover, and cook for about 5 minutes, stirring occasionally, until wilted. Remove from the heat and drain well, pressing out as much liquid as possible, then leave until cool enough to handle. Roughly chop the spinach greens.

Beat the eggs in a bowl, add the feta and dill and season well with black pepper. Add the spinach and stir to combine thoroughly.

Line the baking dish with three layers of phyllo pastry dough, brushing each sheet with butter as you go, and letting the sheets hang over the edge of the dish. Spread the spinach filling in an even layer over the phyllo, then fold up the overhanging dough over it. Top with another three layers of phyllo, brushing each sheet with butter.

Using a sharp knife, mark the top with a diamond pattern, then bake in the oven for about 35 minutes, until crisp and golden. Serve warm or cold.

Spinach and nutmeg soup

SERVES 4

2 tbsp. butter
2 small onions, chopped
1 potato, chopped
4¾ cups vegetable stock
18 oz. spinach
½ cup heavy cream
pinch of freshly grated nutmeg
juice of ¼–½ lemon
salt and freshly ground black pepper

Melt the butter in a large pot, then add the onions and gently fry for about 4 minutes until soft. Add the potato and vegetable stock. Bring to a boil, then reduce the heat, cover, and simmer for about 15 minutes, until the potatoes are tender.

Meanwhile, wash and drain the spinach. Add to the pot and cook over a gentle heat for about 3 minutes, until it has wilted.

Working in batches, tip the contents of the pot into a blender or food processor and blend until smooth. Return to the pot and heat through gently. Stir in the cream, then add the nutmeg and lemon juice and season to taste with salt and pepper. Serve.

NOTES

Garlicky spinach with raisins and pine nuts

SERVES 4

1 tbsp. raisins
2 tbsp. olive oil
6 tbsp. pine nuts
3 cloves garlic, finely chopped
18 oz. spinach, washed and dried
salt and freshly ground black pepper

Place the raisins in a bowl, cover with boiling water, and let soak for about 10 minutes. Drain well and set aside.

Heat the oil in a large pot, add the pine nuts and gently fry for 2-3 minutes until golden. Add the garlic and cook for about 30 seconds, being careful not to let it burn.

Add the spinach to the pot and toss over the heat for about 3 minutes, until it has wilted. Stir in the raisins, season to taste with salt and pepper, and serve immediately.

Roast monkfish on creamy garlic spinach

SERVES 4

1 monkfish tail (about 18 oz.)
2-3 cloves garlic
¼ lemon, cut into slices
2 sprigs of fresh rosemary
salt and freshly ground black pepper
about 2 tbsp. olive oil
2 tbsp. butter
1 lb., 5 oz. spinach, washed and dried
3 tbsp. heavy cream
pinch of freshly grated nutmeg
lemon wedges, for serving

Heat the oven to 425°F. Remove any membrane from the monkfish tail and cut down either side of the central bone to create two fillets.

Finely slice 1½ of the garlic cloves and sprinkle them over the cut side of one of the monkfish fillets, top with the lemon slices and then with the sprigs of rosemary. Place the second fillet, cut-side down, on top to form a fish-fillet "sandwich." Tie together with string to hold securely. Season well with salt and pepper.

Heat about 1 tablespoon of the oil in a frying pan. Add the monkfish "sandwich" and fry for about 2-3 minutes on each side until browned. Transfer to a baking dish, drizzle with a little more oil, and roast in the oven for 15-20 minutes until cooked through.

About 5 minutes before the end of the cooking time, melt the butter in a large pot. Chop the remaining garlic and gently fry in the butter for about 1 minute. Add the spinach and cook, stirring, for about 2 minutes until wilted. Stir in the cream and nutmeg and season to taste with black pepper.

Remove the string from the fish and slice thickly. Serve on top of the creamy spinach, with lemon wedges for squeezing over it.

asparagus

Tender fresh asparagus, with its mild yet distinctive flavor, is one of the great joys of spring, lasting right through into early summer. The green variety is the most common, with stems that can vary in size from fine spears only a fraction of an inch thick to sticks as sturdy as your thumb. You will also come across white and purple-tinged asparagus.

Usually eaten as an appetizer—served warm with melted butter, vinaigrette, or hollandaise sauce—the cooked spears are also a wonderful addition to salads, tarts, layered terrines, risottos, pasta, and even scrambled eggs. They make an attractive and delicious topping for canapés, such as bruschetta and crostini, too.

Asparagus is best eaten on the day it is picked, so it is ideal if you can grow your own or buy it locally from somewhere you know it has been freshly picked. Farm shops are often a good source. Imported asparagus can be tough and lacking in flavor. Look for firm green spears with tightly packed buds, and avoid any that are withered or beginning to brown.

preparing and cooking asparagus

Asparagus spears can be cooked in numerous ways, but the simplest method is to cook them in simmering water until just tender. They can then be eaten with your fingers, accompanied by a dip of melted butter or hollandaise sauce.

Some cooks recommend using an asparagus steamer to cook the spears. This is a tall pot with a basket inside to hold the spears upright, so that when the pan is filled with boiling water, the stalks cook in the water, while the delicate tips steam above it. However, it is just as effective to cook asparagus lying flat in a frying pan containing about an inch of simmering water. Cooking time will depend on the thickness of the spears. If they are thin and delicate, they will become tender in a couple of minutes, while thicker stems may need 6-8 minutes. The best way to test if asparagus is cooked is to lift a spear out with a spatula and take a bite. It should be tender and juicy, but not soft.

To prepare asparagus, rinse lightly under cold running water, then snap off the end of each stem—it should pop and break just where the stem ceases to be woody and becomes tender. Pour about an inch of water into a large frying pan and bring to a boil. Arrange the asparagus in the pan in a single layer and cook over a low-medium heat until tender. Then carefully lift out of the pan using a spatula and pat dry on paper towels before serving.

NOTES

Roast asparagus wrapped in pancetta

SERVES 4

7 oz. thin green asparagus
(about 10-12 spears)
16 wafer-thin slices pancetta,
cut into 2-3 in. strips
olive oil, for drizzling
freshly ground black pepper

FOR THE LEMON MAYONNAISE
½ cup mayonnaise
juice and grated rind of 1 lemon
small handful of fresh dill,
finely chopped

Heat the oven to 375°F.

Prepare the lemon mayonnaide in a small serving bowl by mixing together the mayonnaise, lemon juice and rind, and the chopped dill. Cover and place in the fridge.

Wrap each asparagus spear in a strip of pancetta. Arrange on a baking sheet and drizzle the olive oil over them. Sprinkle a little black pepper on top and roast in the oven for 6-7 minutes until tender.

Serve warm with the bowl of lemon mayonnaise.

Asparagus risotto

SERVES 4

1¾ lb. asparagus, trimmed
3⅓ cups vegetable stock
2 tbsp. butter
1 onion, finely chopped
1½ cups risotto rice
¾ cup vermouth
½ cup grated Parmesan cheese, plus
extra for sprinkling
large handful of fresh flat-leaf
parsley, chopped
1 tsp. chopped fresh mint leaves
salt and freshly ground black pepper

Pour about an inch of water into a large frying pan and bring to a boil. Lower the heat, arrange the asparagus in the pan in a single layer, and then let simmer for about 4 minutes until just tender. Drain, reserving the cooking water. Refresh the spears in cold water, then cut into 2-inch pieces, separating the tips from the stems.

Heat the vegetable stock with the asparagus cooking water in a large pan. Let it simmer gently.

In another large pan, melt the butter, then add the onion and cook gently for about 4 minutes until soft. Add the rice and cook, stirring, for 2 minutes. Pour in the vermouth and cook, stirring, until all the liquid has been absorbed. Add a ladleful of the stock and cook, stirring, until it has been absorbed. Continue cooking and adding stock in this way for about 10 minutes.

Stir in the asparagus stems and continue cooking and adding stock for about 8 minutes. Add the asparagus tips and cook for another 2 minutes, until the rice is tender and creamy.

Remove the pan from the heat and stir in the Parmesan and chopped herbs. Season to taste and serve with extra Parmesan.

artichokes

There are many different varieties of artichoke, ranging from tiny, delicate specimens to huge giants with heads the size of a small cauliflower. Those that arrive with the coming of spring are the first batch of a long growing season that continues right through summer and well into the fall. Piled high on market stalls, these magnificent flower-like vegetables, which are related to the thistle, are almost regal in appearance.

Artichokes are a prized ingredient in many parts of the world, but it is the cuisines of the Mediterranean, where they originate, that have really exploited their subtle taste and texture to the full. Cultivated in Italy since the 15th century, they feature in countless classic Italian dishes: deep-fried and served with pasta, sliced and piled onto pizza, cooked in stews with lamb and salt cod. In Greece, Cyprus, and Turkey, they make a popular side dish, braised with new potatoes and other spring vegetables; and in Morocco they are frequently cooked with preserved lemons and north African spices.

When choosing artichokes, look for green, fresh-looking specimens with the stalk still attached, and avoid those with blemishes or dried-out tips. Store them in the vegetable drawer of the refrigerator and use them as soon as possible after purchase.

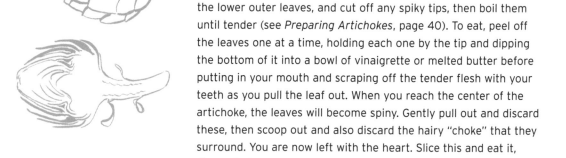

eating artichokes

The simplest way to enjoy artichokes is to cut off the stem, remove the lower outer leaves, and cut off any spiky tips, then boil them until tender (see *Preparing Artichokes*, page 40). To eat, peel off the leaves one at a time, holding each one by the tip and dipping the bottom of it into a bowl of vinaigrette or melted butter before putting in your mouth and scraping off the tender flesh with your teeth as you pull the leaf out. When you reach the center of the artichoke, the leaves will become spiny. Gently pull out and discard these, then scoop out and also discard the hairy "choke" that they surround. You are now left with the heart. Slice this and eat it, dipped in the remaining butter or vinaigrette.

NOTES

preparing artichokes

Artichokes are very versatile and can be prepared in many different ways. The simplest is to cut off the woody stem and the tough outer leaves, then snip off the spiky tops of the remaining leaves and boil whole in salted water—for about 10 minutes for baby ones, and 25–40 minutes for larger specimens. To check if an artichoke is cooked, pull off an outer leaf and bite into the fleshly base—it should be really tender. Drain well and serve, warm or cold, with a dip of garlicky vinaigrette or melted butter (see *Eating Artichokes*, page 38).

Artichokes can also be hollowed out, by removing the hairy choke and fleshly heart, to leave a casing of leaves, ready for stuffing. The choke should be discarded, but the heart makes a lovely addition to stews or braised dishes. Some recipes use only the heart, which can be removed from an uncooked artichoke by cutting away the stalk and larger leaves, then pulling off and discarding the inner leaves. Note that, once cut, artichokes will darken. To avoid this, dip them in a bowl of acidulated water (juice of ½ lemon stirred into 1 quart water) from time to time as you work.

Artichokes dressed in garlic and herbs

SERVES 4

4 large artichokes, stems, outer leaves, and spiky tips of remaining leaves removed
salt and freshly ground black pepper
grated rind of 1 lemon
1 tbsp. lemon juice
1 clove garlic, finely chopped
1 tsp. Dijon mustard
pinch of sugar
3 tbsp. olive oil
handful of fresh flat-leaf parsley, chopped

Cook the artichokes in boiling salted water for 25–40 minutes until cooked (the fleshy bottoms of leaves should be tender). Drain and refresh under cold water. Pat dry with paper towels and set aside.

To make the dressing, whisk together the lemon rind, lemon juice, garlic, mustard, sugar, and olive oil, and season to taste with salt and ground black pepper. Stir in the parsley and set aside.

Cut the artichokes lengthwise into quarters, then use a teaspoon to scoop out the choke and very thin inner leaves. Trim off and discard the woodiest tips of the leaves. Place in a serving bowl, pour the dressing over it, toss to coat, then set aside for at least 30 minutes for the flavors to come together.

NOTES

Artichokes with chicken and preserved lemon

SERVES 4

4 artichokes, stems, outer leaves,
and spiky tips of remaining
leaves removed
3 tbsp. olive oil
4 chicken breasts
2 cloves garlic, chopped
2 tsp. coriander seeds, crushed
1 preserved lemon, chopped
¾ cup white wine
salt and freshly ground black pepper
small handful of fresh flat-leaf
parsley, chopped
couscous, for serving

Cut each artichoke into quarters lengthwise. Remove and discard the choke. Place the artichoke quarters in a bowl of acidulated water (see page 40) and set aside.

Heat 1 tbsp. of the oil in a frying pan. Add the chicken and cook for 1-2 minutes on each side until golden. Set to one side.

Heat the remaining oil in a large saucepan. Add the garlic and cook for 1 minute, stirring. Add the coriander seeds and cook for 30 seconds, then add the drained artichokes, preserved lemon, and chicken. Pour in the wine, season with salt and pepper, and bring to a boil. Reduce the heat and simmer for about 20 minutes, stirring occasionally, until the artichokes are tender and the chicken is cooked through. Check the seasoning, sprinkle with parsley, and serve with couscous.

Linguine with artichokes and smoked salmon

The blend of pale green artichoke hearts and pink strips of smoked salmon makes this simple, creamy pasta dish look stunning. Marinated artichoke hearts from a jar or can may be substituted when fresh artichokes are out of season.

SERVES 4

11 oz. linguine
salt and freshly ground black pepper
½ cup heavy cream
½ cup white wine
1 bunch scallions, shredded
4 large artichoke hearts, cooked
(see *Preparing Artichokes*,
page 40) and chopped
1 tsp. whole-grain mustard
7 oz. smoked salmon, cut into strips
(about 1 cup)

Cook the linguine in boiling salted water according to the instructions on the packet.

About 3 minutes before the end of the pasta cooking time, put the cream, wine, scallions, artichoke hearts, and mustard in a pan and heat gently, stirring to combine.

As soon as the pasta is cooked, drain well. Stir the smoked salmon into the cream mixture, season to taste with salt and pepper, then pour over the pasta and toss well to combine. Serve immediately.

purple sprouting broccoli

In England, the short season for purple sprouting broccoli begins in the depths of winter and continues through into spring. This highly attractive vegetable offers a wonderful alternative to the more commonly found blue-green calabrese variety of broccoli (and the less common bright green romanesco) that is found during the rest of the year. Purple sprouting broccoli has long, shooting stems with coarse green leaves and a purple tinge to its heads. With a more delicate flavor than the other broccolis, it makes a wonderful treat. Enjoy it lightly steamed until tender and served as an appetizer with hollandaise sauce or melted butter (rather like asparagus) or use it in tarts, gratins, soups, sauces, and pasta dishes, as well as in stir-fries and salads.

When buying, always choose firm stems with tightly packed heads and really fresh-looking greens. Avoid specimens that are wilting, soft, or discolored. Remove the leaves, trim the ends of the stalks, and peel away any thick skin, then either steam or boil until it is just tender and still retains its bite and color. If stir-frying, cut into bite-size pieces. If a recipe calls for only the florets, do not throw away the stems—when cooked, they are tender and juicy and have a marvelous flavor. Use them in another recipe such as a soup or stew.

Broccoli and scallion salad

SERVES 4
2 bunches scallions
2 tbsp. olive oil
2¾ lb. purple sprouting broccoli, trimmed
shavings of Parmesan cheese for sprinkling (optional)

FOR THE DRESSING
½ tsp. grated orange rind
½ red chili, seeded and chopped
2 tbsp. orange juice
1 tsp. lemon juice
2 tbsp. olive oil
salt and freshly ground black pepper

First make the dressing. Put all the ingredients in a glass measuring cup, season to taste with salt and pepper, and whisk together. Set aside.

Heat the broiler to hot. Trim the root and tops of the scallions and strip off the papery outer skin. Arrange on a broiler pan. Drizzle with the olive oil and season to taste with salt and pepper. Broil for 3-4 minutes on each side until tender.

Meanwhile, pour about 2inches of water into a wide pan and bring to a boil. Add the broccoli and cook for about 5 minutes, until just tender. Drain well and pat dry.

Divide the broccoli and broiled scallions between four warm serving plates, drizzle the dressing over them, and scatter with Parmesan shavings, if using. Serve immediately.

NOTES

scallions

Scallions (also known as green onions and spring onions), make their first appearance just as the chill of winter starts to recede, and remain available for most of the year. They are immature onions that are harvested only a few months after planting. Creamy white, with fresh green leaves, they can range from long thin stems, about the width of a pencil, to chunky shoots, nearly ½ inch thick, with fat bulbous ends. They have a mild sweet flavor—with none of the pungency of fully grown onions—and a lovely crisp texture that reflects the lush freshness that we associate with the spring harvest.

Trimmed and rinsed under cold running water, they can be left whole, cut into lengths, sliced, chopped, or trimmed to make curls or brushes for garnishes. Raw scallions will enliven a salad or salsa, but they are also delicious cooked. They need only brief cooking, making them a perfect addition to stir-fries and Asian-style soups, into which they can be tossed at the last minute. The really fat scallions are wonderful grilled or broiled, taking on a mouthwatering sweetness as they become succulent and juicy—try serving them with a dip as an appetizer, or tossed into salads.

Grilled scallions with bagna cauda

Brushed with oil, then grilled, scallions take on a deliciously sweet and mellow flavor, far less pungent than they taste when raw. They make the perfect dipper for munching on with this rich, fragrant, garlicky dip from Italy.

SERVES 4
3 bunches fat scallions, trimmed
olive oil, for brushing

FOR THE BAGNA CAUDA
⅔ cup extra virgin olive oil
4 cloves garlic, crushed
2-oz. can anchovy fillets, drained and crushed
⅓ cup (¾ stick) butter
freshly ground black pepper

Heat a grill pan or broiler until hot. Brush the scallions with olive oil. Place on the grill pan or under the hot broiler and cook for about 3 minutes on each side until tender.

Meanwhile, make the bagna cauda. Gently heat the olive oil and garlic in a pan for 2-3 minutes. Stir in the anchovy fillets and butter, and season to taste with black pepper. Put into a serving bowl.

Serve the hot dip immediately with the freshly grilled scallions. If possible, keep the dip warm at the table by placing it in a fondue pan or in a heatproof dish on a tabletop warmer.

NOTES

Hot-and-sour soup with scallions and tofu

The sweet fresh taste of scallions shines through in this intensely flavored broth. Enjoy it as a light appetizer to a Thai-style meal, or stir in a spoonful or two of plain boiled rice or noodles and serve as a light lunch or supper.

SERVES 4

4¾ cups vegetable stock
1 tsp. Thai red curry paste
1 tbsp. sweet chili sauce
2 shallots, finely sliced
2 red chilies, seeded and finely chopped
4 kaffir lime leaves, sliced
1 lemongrass stalk, peeled and finely chopped
1 bunch scallions, trimmed and shredded
2 tbsp. Thai fish sauce
juice of 1 lime
about 2 tsp. soft brown sugar
11 oz. silken tofu, cubed (about 2½-3 cups)
handful of fresh cilantro, chopped

Put the stock, curry paste, sweet chili sauce, shallots, half the chopped chilies, the lime leaves, and lemongrass in a large pot. Bring to a boil, stirring until the curry paste has dissolved, then reduce the heat, cover, and simmer gently for 15 minutes.

Strain the stock into a clean pot. Stir in the scallions, fish sauce, lime juice, and sugar to taste. Bring to a boil, lower the heat, and let simmer for about 1-2 minutes.

Stir in the tofu and cook for another minute, until the tofu is warmed through and the scallions are tender. Sprinkle the remaining chili and the chopped cilantro over it, and serve.

champ

A classic Irish dish, champ is a mixture of creamy mashed potatoes flavored with lightly cooked scallions. It makes a fabulous accompaniment to meat, poultry, and fish.

To prepare, cook about 2 pounds of potatoes (about 8 medium) in lightly salted boiling water for about 20 minutes until tender. Drain well, let them steam dry, then mash.

Trim and finely slice 2 bunches of scallions. Put in a pan with ½ cup of milk and ¼ cup (½ stick) of butter. Heat until bubbling gently, then let simmer for 2-3 minutes.

Stir into the mashed potatoes with 2 tablespoons of crème fraîche or sour cream. Season to taste with salt and freshly ground black pepper and serve piping hot.

garlic

Although available dried at any time of the year, fresh and wild garlic are among the delights of spring. The green young leaves of wild garlic, also known as ramsons, have a powerful and distinctive aroma. Their flavor, however, is no stronger than that of cultivated garlic. They are delicious in salads with other spring salad greens, or shredded and added to soups, stews, risottos, and omelets, or wrapped around fish or meat before broiling or roasting. The bulbs can be used in the same way as those of cultivated garlic.

Fresh, greeny-white bulbs of spring garlic do not reach the market until late in the season. They may be pure white or tinged with purple, depending upon variety, and have a milder, sweeter flavor than dried bulbs, which makes them ideal for roasting whole and using raw in salads.

Almost every cuisine in the world uses garlic in its recipes, from the fragrant dishes of the Mediterranean to the fiery curries of India and Thailand and the subtly spiced stews of the Middle East. Preparation is all important. The more finely you chop garlic, the more pungent its flavor becomes—so for a milder result, cook the bulbs or cloves whole, or for a more intense flavor, crush the peeled cloves. The easiest way to peel garlic is to lay a clove on a board and press down on it with the flat side of a knife blade. The papery skin will split and can then be pulled off.

spaghetti with garlic and chili

This simple Italian dish known as *spaghetti aglio e olio* is the perfect way to show off garlic at its best.

For four people, cook 11 ounces of dried spaghetti in boiling salted water according to the instructions on the package.

Meanwhile, gently heat 5 tablespoons of olive oil in a frying pan. Add 3 crushed cloves of garlic and 1 dried red chili and fry for about 2 minutes, until the garlic gives off its aroma and is just starting to brown. Remove from the heat and discard the chili.

Drain the pasta, stir in the garlicky oil, and scatter a handful of chopped fresh parsley over it. Toss to combine and serve.

NOTES

aioli

This thick, buttery garlic mayonnaise is wonderful served with almost anything—spooned over new potatoes, asparagus spears, or thin florets of purple sprouting broccoli; as a dip with fries or raw vegetables; spread on crostini; or served with salad or poached fish. You can make it at any time of year, but it is at its best prepared with fresh spring garlic. Just combine 2 crushed garlic cloves with 2 egg yolks. Using a blender, gradually beat in about ½ cup of extra virgin olive oil—adding it drop by drop at first, then in a thin drizzle—until the mixture is really thick. Blend in 1 tablespoon of lemon juice and ½ teaspoon of Dijon mustard, then gradually beat in another ½ cup of olive oil and season to taste with salt and freshly ground black pepper. Add a little more lemon juice if you like.

Garlic mussels in white wine

This simple-to-prepare dish is an absolute classic and is one of the best ways to enjoy garlic as an aromatic seasoning. Eat the mussels first, then mop up the rich, garlicky cooking liquor with chunks of crusty French bread.

SERVES 4

4 lb. fresh mussels, cleaned
2 tbsp. butter
3 cloves garlic, finely chopped
1½ cups white wine
6 tbsp. heavy cream
large handful of fresh flat-leaf parsley, roughly chopped
salt and freshly ground black pepper
crusty French bread, for serving

Check the mussels and discard any that are open and do not shut when tapped hard. Melt the butter in a large pot, add the garlic, and gently fry for about 1 minute.

Add the mussels, pour in the wine, cover the pot tightly, and cook for about 5 minutes until the mussels have opened (discard any that haven't opened).

Lift the mussels into warmed serving bowls using a slotted spoon. Quickly stir the cream and chopped parsley into the cooking liquor and season with salt and pepper to taste. Pour the sauce over the mussels and serve with the crusty French bread.

NOTES

Chicken with forty cloves of garlic

Garlic can be used as a vegetable in its own right, roasted whole to produce a sweet, mellow result—and you can easily allow a whole bulb per person without the flavor being overwhelming. Cooked in this way, the flesh becomes mild, fragrant, smooth, and buttery and can be squeezed out of the papery skin. Roast cloves of garlic make a delicious partner for roast chicken, as in this recipe, but are also good simply spread on crusty bread or thin slices of warm toast and eaten as a snack.

SERVES 4-6

1 lemon
3½-lb. free-range chicken
4-6 sprigs of fresh thyme
about 2 tbsp. butter
salt and freshly ground black pepper
5 bulbs garlic
about 2 tbsp. olive oil
1 cup chicken stock
2 tbsp. white wine

Heat the oven to 400°F.

Cut the lemon in half and rub the cut ends all over the chicken, then place the lemon halves in the cavity of the bird along with the thyme. Rub the butter all over the breasts and legs, and season well with salt and pepper. Place the chicken in a roasting pan.

Remove the papery outer layers of skin from the garlic bulbs, leaving them whole, then slice off the very tops to expose the cloves. Place the bulbs on a large sheet of foil, drizzle the oil over them, season with a little salt and pepper, then fold up the foil tightly around them and place in the roasting pan next to the chicken.

Roast in the oven for 45 minutes. Remove from the oven and unwrap the garlic, discarding the foil. Tuck the garlic in around the chicken, drizzling over them any juices that have formed. Return to the oven and cook for another 15 minutes until golden. Insert the point of a knife into the thickest part of the thigh—if the juices run clear, the chicken is cooked; if not, return to the oven for another 15 minutes, then check again. Transfer the cooked chicken and garlic to a board and let it rest for 10 minutes.

Meanwhile, make the gravy. Skim off the fat from the juices left in the roasting pan and discard, then pour the juices into a blender. Squeeze the flesh from 2 of the bulbs of garlic and also add to the blender. Pour in the chicken stock and wine and blend until smooth. Pour into a saucepan, heat through, and serve with the chicken and remaining roasted garlic bulbs.

avocados

Native to South America, the avocado grows in most tropical regions of the world. With different varieties coming into season at different times, they are available most of the year—but their fresh flavor and delightful, pale green, buttery flesh seems so at home on the spring table with the green, tender shoots and stems of that season. Color, flavor, and texture vary according to variety. The skin ranges from bright green and shiny to purple-black and knobbly, but all types have a rich, creamy flesh when ripe.

Avocado flesh is fabulous in salsas or tossed into salads and makes a good, enriching addition when blended into soups and smoothies. However, it starts to blacken quite quickly once exposed to the air, so prepare avocados only shortly before serving. Squeeze lemon juice on any leftover avocado and cover closely with plastic wrap to prevent it discoloring.

Avocado salad with spicy seared shrimp (opposite)

SERVES 4

2 tbsp. sweet chili sauce
1 tsp. soy sauce
juice of 1 lime
1 clove garlic, crushed
10 oz. raw tiger shrimp, peeled
(leaving tails on) and deveined
2 large handfuls of mixed
spring greens, such as arugula
and baby spinach
2 avocados, peeled, pitted, and cut
into bite-size chunks
4 scallions, trimmed and sliced

FOR THE DRESSING

juice and grated rind of 1 lime
1½ tsp. soft brown sugar
2 tbsp. sunflower oil
½ red chili, seeded and chopped
2 tsp. chopped fresh mint leaves
salt

Combine the chili sauce, soy sauce, lime juice, and garlic in a bowl. Add the shrimp, toss to coat, then leave in the fridge to marinate for at least 30 minutes.

Meanwhile, whisk together the dressing ingredients in a glass measuring cup, seasoning to taste with salt. Set aside.

Divide the salad greens among individual serving plates or bowls. Scatter the avocado chunks and scallions over the greens, then drizzle about two-thirds of the dressing over them and toss to coat the greens.

Heat a ridged grill pan or broiler until hot, and use to cook the shrimp, with any marinade poured over them, for about 1–2 minutes on each side, until pink and cooked through. Scatter the hot shrimp over the plates of salad, drizzle the remaining dressing over them, and serve immediately.

NOTES

rhubarb

"Forced" rhubarb—cultivated in dark sheds to encourage the stems to grow in the search for light —arrives at the end of winter. Naturally-grown rhubarb appears in early spring and lasts to the beginning of summer. It is brighter in color with a stronger flavor than the forced variety and makes a real treat, as one of the first of the seasonal fruits to reach the market.

Choose forced rhubarb with firm pink stems and no trace of green or soft slimy patches. Naturally-grown rhubarb is green and pink-red in color, but again go for firm fresh-looking stems. To prepare, cut off and discard the leaves and woody stem tips, then strip out any tough strings and cut into chunks. Simmer in a covered pan with sugar and very little water, or sprinkle with sugar and bake.

Rhubarb meringue pie

SERVES 6
11 oz. rhubarb, trimmed
and chopped
1 tsp. ground cinnamon
¾ cup sugar
2 eggs, separated

FOR THE PIE DOUGH
generous ¾ cup all-purpose flour
½ tbsp. sugar
¼ cup (½ stick) butter, chilled and
cut up
about 1 tbsp. cold water

Make the dough. Put the flour and sugar in a food processor and pulse to combine. Add the butter and blend until the mixture resembles fine bread crumbs. With the machine running, add just enough water for the mixture to come together. Lightly press the dough into a ball, wrap in plastic wrap, and chill for 30 minutes.

Heat the oven to 375°F. Put the rhubarb, cinnamon, and 3 tablespoons of the sugar in a pan, cover, and heat gently, shaking occasionally, until the juices flow. Increase the heat slightly and simmer for 6-8 minutes until the rhubarb is tender. Remove from the heat, beat in the egg yolks, one at a time, then let it cook gently, stirring, for 2-3 minutes until thickened. Set aside.

Bake the crust first. Roll out the dough to line an 8-inch pie plate. Cover with foil, scatter in some baking beans, and bake in the oven for 10 minutes. Remove the beans and foil, then bake for 5-10 minutes more, until crisp and golden. Meanwhile, beat the egg whites to form stiff peaks. Fold in the remaining sugar, a spoonful at a time, to make a meringue.

Pour the rhubarb mixture into the pie crust and spread out in an even layer. Swirl the meringue on top, then bake for 20-25 minutes until golden. Serve hot or warm.

NOTES

carrots

Although carrots that have been kept in cold-storage are available at almost any time, the first carrots of the year arrive at the end of spring, with the main harvest at the end of summer or early autumn. These sweet, bright-orange roots are delicious eaten raw or cooked. Sliced, chopped, grated or cut into thin sticks, they can be transformed into wonderful salads or added to soups, stews, curries, and even some desserts, such as carrot cake with cream cheese frosting. In India, grated carrots are cooked slowly with milk, sugar, and spices to make that wonderful, sticky, fudgy sweet, *halwa*. They are also excellent boiled and mashed with rutabagas, turnips, or potatoes, and plenty of butter, or roasted along with a selection of other root vegetables, or juiced with a knob of fresh ginger root, then served up blended with orange or apple juice.

When buying carrots, look for firm unblemished specimens, ideally with fresh-looking leaves attached. Look out too for those that have been organically grown, as they tend to have the best flavor. If using organic carrots, just trim and scrub well to prepare, leaving the skins on, as this is where much of the flavor resides. Non-organic carrots are best peeled.

Carrots are best cooked in very little liquid, so that all their flavor stays inside rather than being lost in the cooking liquid. The simplest way is to slice them thinly and cook in a covered pan with just a splash of water, a pat of butter, and a good grinding of salt and pepper, until tender and sweet. If there is any liquid left in the pan when the carrots are cooked, increase the heat and cook uncovered, stirring, until it has all evaporated.

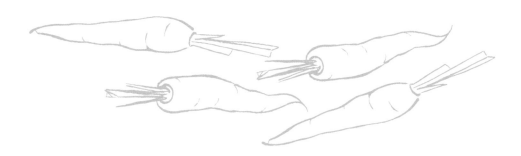

NOTES

Sea bass baked on gingered carrots

Baking carrots brings out their intense sweetness, which is enhanced and balanced here by the addition of pungent fresh ginger and the zesty tang of fresh lime juice. This creates a strongly flavored bed of vegetables that is the perfect foil for the mild-tasting sea bass.

SERVES 4

4 sea bass fillets, about 6 oz. each
salt and freshly ground black pepper
juice of 2 limes
2 tbsp. sunflower oil
1 onion, finely chopped
1 clove garlic, crushed
1-inch piece fresh ginger, peeled and grated
1½ lb. carrots, grated

Heat the oven to 450°F. Season the fish well with salt and pepper, sprinkle the lime juice over it and set aside.

Heat the oil in a large pan. Add the onion, garlic, and ginger and fry gently for about 5 minutes until soft. Add the carrots and cook, stirring, for about 5 minutes until just tender. Remove from the heat. Pour in the lime juice from the fish and season to taste with salt and pepper.

Transfer the carrot mixture to a baking dish, then arrange the fish fillets in a single layer on top, skin side up. Bake in the oven for about 10 minutes until the fish is just cooked through.

moroccan-style carrot dip

Cooked carrot salads, flavored with warm spices such as cumin, ginger, and chili, are popular throughout North Africa. This aromatic, fiery-colored dip has similar flavorings and is great served with wedges of pita bread for scooping, either on its own as an appetizer or as part of a selection of snacks or *mezze* nibbles, such as hummus, stuffed vine greens, and olives.

To make, just peel and slice 1 pound of carrots and put in a pan with 3 tablespoons of cold water, then bring to a boil, lower the heat, and simmer gently for 25-30 minutes, shaking the pan from time to time, until the carrots are soft. If there is still cooking liquid in the pan, increase the heat and let it bubble, stirring, until most of it has evaporated.

Transfer the cooked carrots to a food processor with 1½ chopped garlic cloves, 1 teaspoon of grated fresh ginger, a good pinch of cayenne pepper, 1 teaspoon each of ground cumin and ground corianter, 1 tablespoon of red wine vinegar, 2½ tablespoons of olive oil, and a good pinch of salt.

Blend to form a smooth purée, check the seasoning, and add a little more salt and cayenne pepper if needed. Scoop into a bowl and chill well before serving.

Carrot and cardamom cake *(opposite)*

Carrots have a natural affinity with warm spices such as ginger, cinnamon, and cardamom, and their intense sugary flavor makes them an ideal candidate for sweet dishes and desserts. Stirred into cake batter, they produce a deliciously moist cake that keeps well.

MAKES 1 LARGE CAKE
½ cup soft brown sugar
¼ cup granulated sugar
1 cup sunflower oil
3 eggs
grated rind of 1 orange
seeds from 10 cardamom pods, crushed
½ tsp. ground ginger
2¼ cups all-purpose flour
3 tsp. baking powder
1 tsp. salt
2 large carrots, grated (about 1⅔ cups grated)
¾ cup chopped walnuts

FOR THE FROSTING
1 cup mascarpone cheese
grated rind of 1 orange
2 tsp. lemon juice
½ cup confectioners' sugar

Heat the oven to 350°F. Grease an 8-inch round cake pan and dust it with flour.

Beat together the sugars, oil, and eggs in a large bowl, then stir in the orange rind, cardamom seeds, and ginger. Sift in the flour and carefully fold in, then fold in the grated carrots and walnuts. Tip the mixture into the prepared cake pan and spread out evenly. Bake for 1-1¼ hours in the oven, until a skewer inserted in the center comes out clean. Turn out onto a wire rack and let cool completely.

To make the frosting, beat together the mascarpone, orange rind, lemon juice, and confectioners' sugar. Spread over the cooled cake. Serve cut into wedges.

baked carrots

This simple technique produces a similar result to cooking carrots in a pan with very little water. Allow 1-2 carrots per person. Cut them into sticks or diagonal slices and place in the center of a large square of foil. Season to taste with salt and freshly ground black pepper, dot with a pat or two of butter, and drizzle over them ½-1 tablespoon of vermouth (per serving). Wrap the foil around the carrots and twist the ends to make a well-sealed package. Place on a baking tray and bake in a heated oven at 375°F for 15-20 minutes, until sweet and tender. If you like, sprinkle a handful of freshly chopped seasonal herbs over them just before serving.

new potatoes

Although potatoes are available all year round and are a common staple in many national cuisines, the arrival of tiny new potatoes in spring is a real treat. Sweet and tender, most varieties are best eaten in their skins, where much of their nutritional value and flavor lies.

When buying, choose unblemished potatoes and, if you can find them, buy ones that are still covered in muddy soil. Wash well, removing any bad spots, but never peel them. Larger new potatoes can be cut in half, but leave the smaller ones whole. Then simply boil in salted water for about 15 minutes, or until tender.

With their waxy flesh, boiled new potatoes are perfect for using in salads—either warm or cold. Try tossing them, fresh from the pan, into a bowl of baby spinach, along with chunks of Gorgonzola cheese; the heat of the potatoes will wilt the leaves and melt the cheese, producing a sublimely indulgent dish. Or boil and lightly crush the potatoes, then serve with a sprinkling of freshly chopped spring herbs and a drizzle of extra virgin olive oil; or parboil, then toss in olive oil, sprinkle with sea salt, and roast until crisp.

New potatoes cooked with onion and garlic

SERVES 4
2 tbsp. butter
1 onion, finely chopped
2 cloves garlic, finely chopped
1½ lb. new potatoes, cut in half
salt and freshly ground black pepper
¼ cup water
handful of fresh flat-leaf parsley or chives, chopped

Melt the butter in a pan. Add the onion and garlic and cook gently over a low heat for about 4 minutes, until soft. Add the potatoes, season to taste with salt and pepper, toss to combine, then pour in the water and cover the pan tightly.

Let it simmer gently, shaking the pan from time to time, for about 15 minutes, until the potatoes are tender and the liquid reduced. Check the level of liquid in the pan towards the end of cooking and add a splash more water if it is too dry. Toss in the chopped herbs, check the seasoning, and serve.

NOTES

Chicken and new potato stew with chorizo and sherry

SERVES 4

2 tbsp. olive oil
4 chicken breasts or legs, about 7 oz. each
1 onion, cut in half and sliced
2 cloves garlic
2 oz. chorizo, cut up
14½-oz. can chopped tomatoes
½ cup dry sherry
pinch of dried red pepper flakes
salt
1 lb. new potatoes
handful of fresh flat-leaf parsley, chopped

Heat the oil in a large wide pan, add the chicken, and brown all over. Remove from the pan and set aside.

Reduce the heat under the pan, add the onion and garlic, and cook for about 5 minutes, until soft. Add the chorizo and cook for 2 minutes, then add the tomatoes, sherry, and red pepper flakes, and season with a little salt.

Add the browned chicken and the potatoes to the pan, bring to a boil, then reduce the heat even more, cover, and let simmer gently for 25–30 minutes, stirring occasionally, until the chicken is cooked through and the potatoes tender. Check the seasoning and serve sprinkled with the chopped parsley.

new potato salad

Cooked in their skins, bite-size new potatoes, with their wonderful waxy texture and earthy flavor, are perfect for making into potato salad. This recipe can be served warm or at room temperature.

For four, allow about 1½ pounds of potatoes. Scrub them clean, cut any large ones in half, then cook in boiling salted water for about 10 minutes until tender. Drain well and let them steam dry.

Meanwhile, make the dressing. Pound 2 peeled garlic cloves in a mortar, then work in 1 teaspoon of Dijon mustard and about 1½ tablespoons of sherry vinegar (use white wine vinegar, if unavailable). Whisk in ¼ cup of extra virgin olive oil, a handful of fresh flat-leaf parsley, and a few sprigs of fresh mint, both finely chopped. Season with plenty of freshly ground black pepper and a little salt.

Pour the dressing over the cooked potatoes, toss to mix in thoroughly, and serve.

morels

Morels—unlike most other wild mushrooms which appear in the fall—are a springtime delicacy. Pale brown, with creamy white flesh, their wrinkly pointed caps resemble a sponge. The short stems are hollow inside and should always be split and rinsed under cold running water to remove dirt and dust before using. Morels have an intense aroma and flavor that goes particularly well with butter and cream, and are considered a real gourmet treat. They make a good addition to risottos and sauces.

Morels should never be eaten raw and generally require longer cooking than other mushrooms. First split them in half and wash as described above, then sauté in butter for about 30 minutes until tender and juicy. If you are lucky enough to find yourself with a glut of morels, they can be threaded on string and dried, then stored in an airtight container. Soak dried morels in warm water for about 20 minutes before cooking.

Creamy morels on polenta wedges *(opposite)*

SERVES 6
2 tbsp. butter
1 large clove garlic, crushed
8 oz. fresh morels, or a mixture of morels and cultivated mushrooms, cleaned (see above)
3 tbsp. white wine
salt and freshly ground black pepper
2 tbsp. heavy cream
handful of fresh flat-leaf parsley, chopped, plus extra for sprinkling

FOR THE WEDGES
2 cups water
¾ cup quick-cook polenta (cornmeal)
butter, for frying

First make the wedges. Bring the water to a boil in a large pan, add a pinch of salt and then the polenta, stirring constantly. Continue cooking for about 3 minutes until the mixture is really thick, then turn it out onto a wooden board in a mound, flatten down slightly till it's ½-inch thick, and let it cool and set. When set, cut into six wedges and set aside.

Melt the butter in a clean pan, add the garlic, and fry gently for 1 minute. Add the mushrooms and wine, season with a little salt, and cook over a low heat for 25 minutes, stirring occasionally, until tender and the liquid has evaporated. Stir in the cream and parsley and season to taste with salt and pepper.

Melt a little butter in a frying pan (with a ridged bottom, if available), add the polenta wedges, and fry on both sides until crisp and golden. Top each one with a spoonful of the mushrooms, sprinkle a little extra parsley on top, and serve immediately.

NOTES

lamb

Lamb is available at any time of the year, but the sweet, succulent, tender meat from animals aged between 4 and 12 months is traditionally associated with spring. Simply roasted with garlic and rosemary, and served with mint sauce, new potatoes, and carrots, lamb makes a truly special seasonal feast.

But it is not just the roasting cuts, such as the leg, shoulder, saddle, loin, and rack, that can be enjoyed in spring; there is also a fabulous choice of smaller cuts that can be pan-fried or broiled for a quick, easily prepared weekday meal. Try loin and sirloin chops, or tender leg steaks, cutlets, or ribs. Tougher cuts, such as shank and neck, make wonderful stews, and cubed or ground lamb is perfect in pies, stuffed vegetables, and baked dishes, such as *moussaka*.

When choosing lamb, look for firm pink meat with a firm-grained texture and creamy white fat. Avoid dark, grainy, or dry-looking meat, or meat with yellowing fat.

marinades for lamb

One of the best ways to prepare small cuts of lamb, such as leg steaks, chops, and cutlets, is to marinate them for at least 1 hour in the fridge, then broil or pan-fry. Simple marinades include:

2 crushed cloves of garlic mixed with 2 tablespoons of red wine vinegar, a few sprigs of chopped fresh thyme or oregano, and 1 tablespoon of olive oil, then seasoned with salt and black pepper.

2 crushed cloves of garlic mixed with the juice of 1 lemon, 2 teaspoons of ground cumin, 1 teaspoon of ground coriander, 1 tablespoon of olive oil, and salt and black pepper to taste.

2 crushed cloves of garlic mixed with ½ finely chopped onion, a small handful of chopped fresh cilantro or mint, 1 teaspoon of chili powder, ½ cup of plain yogurt, and salt and black pepper to taste.

NOTES

Roast lamb with rosemary, garlic, and white beans

SERVES 4-6

1¼ cups dried navy beans, soaked in cold water overnight
1 leg of lamb, about 4 lb.
4 cloves garlic, 2 slivered and 2 finely chopped
5 sprigs of fresh rosemary
¼ cup olive oil
salt and freshly ground black pepper
1 onion, finely chopped
3 strips of bacon, cut into small pieces
2 cups lamb or beef stock
1 cup boiling water
½ cup white wine
1 bay leaf

Drain the beans, rinse well, and place in a large pot. Cover with cold water and bring to a boil. Boil rapidly for about 10 minutes and skim off any scum that floats to the surface. Reduce the heat and let it simmer for about 45 minutes, until the beans are just tender, but not soft. Drain and set aside.

Meanwhile, with a small knife, make slits all over the lamb, then press the garlic slivers, and the leaves from 2 of the rosemary sprigs into the slits. Drizzle about half the oil over the lamb and season well with salt and pepper. Set aside.

Heat the oven to 375°F. Heat the remaining oil in a pan, add the onion and chopped garlic, and cook over a gentle heat for about 5 minutes, until soft. Add the bacon and cooked beans, and toss to combine. Tip the mixture into a large roasting pan or baking dish. Pour in the stock, water, and wine, and tuck in the remaining rosemary and the bay leaf.

Place the lamb on top of the beans and roast it in the oven for about 2 hours, or until the meat is cooked to your liking. Let it rest for about 15 minutes before carving, keeping the beans warm to serve with the lamb.

Lamb tagine with dried apricots

SERVES 4

18 oz. lamb shoulder, cut into 1-inch cubes
1 onion, thinly sliced
2 cloves garlic, chopped
pinch of ground ginger
1 tsp. ground cinnamon
2 tsp. ground cumin
2 tbsp. olive oil
⅔ cup ready-to-eat dried apricots
juice of ½ lemon
salt and freshly ground black pepper
couscous, for serving

Put the lamb, onion, garlic, ginger, cinnamon, cumin, and oil in a heavy pot, season well, and pour in enough cold water to cover. Bring to a boil, then reduce the heat, cover tightly, and let simmer gently for 1 hour.

Stir in the apricots, cover it again, and let simmer for another 30 minutes, until the sauce is reduced and the lamb is tender. Stir occasionally towards the end of cooking to prevent the bottom of the stew from burning, and add a splash more water if it is becoming too dry. Stir in the lemon juice, season to taste with salt and pepper, and serve with couscous.

Summer

Along with rising temperatures comes a wealth of vibrant fresh ingredients that all depend upon long days of warmth and sunlight to develop their full flavor. Tender lettuce leaves, crunchy cucumbers, sweet-tasting peas, ears of golden corn, and crisp green beans all mark the arrival of summer, as do offerings associated with the sunny Mediterranean, such as tomatoes, sweet bell peppers, tender zucchinis, and fat glossy eggplants. Fruit, too, is one of the glories of the season. After the relative austerity of winter and spring, the arrival of an abundance of glistening summer fruits, piled high on market stalls and produce stands, is a pleasure to relish. Juicy cherries, berries in varied tones of red and purple, and heavily scented melons ripen to perfection under the sun's rays to achieve their intense sweetness. Velvet-skinned peaches and nectarines just cry out to be bitten into, and the sharp intensity of gooseberries and the honeyed tang of fresh apricots are utterly irresistible, eaten fresh or blended into mouth-tingling purees and mousses.

summer herbs

As the warmer weather continues into summer, an abundance of fragrant herbs appears. The heady perfume of cilantro, mint, basil, tarragon, dill, chives, parsley, and marjoram should fill the summer kitchen. Toss into salads or use as flavorings and garnishes for cooked dishes. Create delicious herb butters to spoon onto potatoes or roasted onions or grilled fish and meat. These can be made very quickly and easily: simply chop up a large handful of fresh herbs and blend with a few tablespoons of softened butter, then season with freshly ground black pepper.

Couscous with summer vegetables and herbs (opposite)

This simple salad of couscous, sweet roasted vegetables, and salty feta cheese, infused with the intense aromas of fresh mint, parsley, and basil, makes a wonderful light meal or side dish with grilled meat or fish. Prepare in advance to serve at summer picnics or barbecues.

SERVES 4

2 yellow bell peppers, cut into large chunks
2 red bell peppers, cut into large chunks
9 oz. cherry tomatoes
2 zucchinis, thickly sliced
5 tbsp. olive oil
salt and freshly ground black pepper
1 tbsp. white wine vinegar
1 tsp. Dijon mustard
pinch of sugar
1 cup couscous
1 cup boiling water
4 oz. feta cheese, crumbled (about 1 cup)
1 tbsp. chopped fresh mint leaves
large handful of fresh flat-leaf parsley, chopped
handful of fresh basil leaves, torn

Heat the oven to 400°F. Put the bell peppers, tomatoes, and zucchinis in a large baking dish, drizzle 2 tablespoons of the oil over them, season well with salt and pepper, and toss to coat. Roast in the oven for about 30 minutes, tossing once or twice, until tender and slightly charred.

Meanwhile, prepare the dressing. Whisk together the vinegar, mustard, sugar, and 2½ tablespoons of the oil, and season to taste with salt and pepper, then set aside.

Put the couscous in a large bowl, blend in the remaining oil and a pinch of salt using a fork, then pour in the boiling water. Let it stand for 5 minutes, then fluff up with a fork.

Add the roasted vegetables and any juices from the dish to the couscous along with the feta, and sprinkle wth the mint, parsley, and basil. Pour in the dressing, then toss to combine well and serve either warm or at room temperature.

NOTES

Pesto with trenette, potatoes, and green beans

SERVES 4

2 large handfuls of fresh
basil leaves
⅓ cup pine nuts
1 clove garlic, chopped
¼ cup olive oil
½ cup grated Parmesan cheese, plus
extra for serving
salt and freshly ground black pepper
11 oz. dried trenette noodles or
fettucine
about 9 oz. potatoes, chopped
11 oz. green beans, trimmed and cut
in half if long

First make the pesto. Put the basil, pine nuts, and garlic in a food processor or blender with half of the oil and blend briefly to mix. Scrape down the sides, add the remaining oil, and blend some more, until smooth. Stir in the Parmesan and season to taste with black pepper. Set aside.

Cook the noodles in a pan of boiling salted water according to the instructions on the package. Five minutes before the end of cooking time, add the potatoes and beans, and cook until tender. Drain well, reserving about ¼ cup of the water.

Stir the reserved water into the pesto, then pour the mixture over the pasta and vegetables. Toss to combine, and serve immediately, sprinkled with more Parmesan and black pepper.

Herb-marinated pork steaks

The tangy Asian-inspired marinade is brimming with the fragrances of lemongrass, lime zest, and cilantro. Serve this quick-to-prepare dish with a salad of summer greens, tossed together with ripe tomatoes, crunchy cucumbers, and a few chunks of ripe peach or mango.

SERVES 4

4 pork loin steaks
2 lemongrass stalks, chopped
2 cloves garlic, crushed
3-inch piece fresh ginger, peeled
and grated
1 green chili, seeded and
finely chopped
handful of fresh cilantro, chopped
grated rind and juice of 2 limes
2 tsp. soy sauce
2 tbsp. sunflower oil

Arrange the pork steaks in a single layer in a dish. Combine the lemongrass, garlic, ginger, chili, cilantro, lime rind and juice, soy sauce, and oil in a bowl, then pour it over the steaks, turning them to coat well. Leave to marinate in the fridge for at least 1 hour.

Heat the broiler to hot. Lift the steaks out of the marinade and arrange on a broiler pan. Pour the marinade over them, then cook under the broiler for about 6 minutes on each side, until just cooked through. Serve immediately.

NOTES

Fish en papillote with summer herbs

SERVES 4

2 tbsp. olive oil
1 onion, halved and sliced
2 cloves garlic, finely chopped
2 zucchinis, cut into sticks
2 yellow bell peppers, cut into strips
salt and freshly ground black pepper
2 handfuls of fresh basil, chopped
1 tbsp. chopped fresh mint leaves
4 salmon fillets, about 6 oz. each, skinned
juice of 1 lemon

Heat the oven to 400°F. Cut out four 14-inch squares of greaseproof paper or foil.

Heat the oil in a large frying pan. Add the onion and garlic and fry gently for about 5 minutes until soft. Increase the heat, toss in the zucchinis and peppers, and cook, stirring frequently, for another 5 minutes. Remove the pan from the heat, season to taste with salt and pepper, then toss in the basil and mint.

Divide the vegetables among the four sheets of paper or foil, placing them in the center. Lay a salmon fillet on top of each pile of vegetables, sprinkle the lemon juice over it, and season with salt and pepper. Scrunch up the paper or foil to form a tightly sealed package. Place on a baking sheet and bake in the oven for about 15 minutes until the fish is cooked. Serve immediately.

Herb omelet

SERVES 2

4 eggs
handful of fresh flat-leaf parsley, chopped
1 tbsp. chopped fresh chives
handful of fresh basil, chopped
salt and freshly ground black pepper
1 tbsp. olive oil

Beat the eggs and chopped herbs together in a large bowl and season well with salt and pepper. Heat the oil in a nonstick frying pan until very hot, then pour in the egg mixture, tilting the pan so that the mixture covers the bottom.

Cook for a few moments until the egg starts to set, then carefully push in the sides of the omelet to allow any uncooked mixture to run onto the bottom of the pan. Cook for another minute or 2, until the egg is just beginning to set on top.

Using a spatula, fold one side of the omelet inwards, then fold the other side over the top of that. Gently cut in half and slide each portion onto a warm serving plate. Serve immediately.

summer salad greens

Summer is the time for lettuces in all their wondrous forms. They are perfect for munching on when the weather is hot and sunny. From pale loose-leafed butterheads (Boston lettuce) and crisp refreshing icebergs to soft leafy lollo rosso lettuce, oakleaf, and corn salad (mâche) and the sweetly flavored romaine and Bibb lettuce, there is such a huge choice available. And there are also the greens that give your salads bite and pep, including peppery chicory, arugula and watercress, and zesty sorrel and wild dandelion. Be adventurous, combining greens in your salads to create a fabulous array of colors, textures, and flavors. Vary them to match the character of other dishes on the table.

Summer greens with charbroiled chicken (opposite)

SERVES 4

1 clove garlic, crushed
pinch of dried red pepper flakes
juice of ½ lemon
4 tbsp. olive oil
salt and freshly ground black pepper
4 chicken breasts, about 7 oz. each,
cut into bite-size pieces
1 tbsp. red wine vinegar
1 tsp. Dijon mustard
2 tsp. chopped fresh mint leaves
2 Bibb lettuces
2 small ripe mangoes, pitted, peeled,
and chopped
1 English cucumber, sliced

Combine the garlic, red pepper flakes, lemon juice, and 1 tablespoon of the olive oil in a large dish and season with a pinch of salt. Add the chicken, toss to coat well, and let marinate in the fridge for at least 1 hour.

Meanwhile, make a dressing by whisking together the remaining olive oil, vinegar, mustard, and mint in a small bowl. Set aside.

Divide the lettuces into leaves, then tear into bite-size chunks. Divide between 4 serving plates or salad bowls. Scatter the mangoes and cucumber on top.

Drain the chicken. Heat a grill pan or broiler until hot and cook the chicken pieces for about 2 minutes on each side, until cooked through. Scatter the hot chicken over the salad, drizzle the dressing over it, and toss to combine. Serve.

NOTES

simple leaf salad

Mixing mildly flavored greens and flavorsome herbs in a simple salad creates a great accompaniment to summer meals. For four people, combine about 2 large handfuls of summer salad greens, such as corn salad (mâche), oakleaf, lollo rosso lettuce, and chicory, in a large salad bowl. Scatter 2 large handfuls of mixed herbs, such as dill, basil, fennel, mint, chives, cilantro, and flat-leaf parsley, roughly chopped. (Be sparing with the more intensely flavored herbs such as mint and chives.) Whisk together 1½ tablespoons of balsamic vinegar, ¼ cup of olive oil and 1 teaspoon of whole-grain mustard in a small bowl. Season to taste with salt and pepper, drizzle it over the salad, and toss to combine. Serve immediately.

Summer greens salad with smoked salmon

SERVES 4

2 red bell peppers, cut in half lengthwise
4 lightly smoked salmon fillets, about 5 oz. each, skinned
salt and freshly ground black pepper
a very large handful of snow peas
2 large handfuls mixed summer greens, such as arugula, baby spinach, and romaine lettuce
4 tomatoes, cut into eighths
½ English cucumber, sliced
1 tbsp. finely chopped fresh mint leaves
juice of 1 lemon
grated rind of ¼ lemon
3 tbsp. olive oil

Heat the oven to 450°F. Place the peppers, cut side down, on a baking sheet and roast in the oven for about 30 minutes, until blackened all over. Transfer to a bowl, cover with plastic wrap, and let cool for about 10 minutes. Peel, discard the seeds, and cut the flesh into strips. Set aside.

Reduce the oven temperature to 400°F. Arrange the salmon in a baking dish. Season with pepper and bake in the oven for about 9 minutes, until just cooked through.

Meanwhile, cook the snow peas in boiling water for 3 minutes, then drain and refresh under cold water. Drain well and set aside.

Divide the salad greens between four serving plates, and scatter the peppers, tomatoes, cucumber, and snow peas over them. Make a dressing by whisking together the mint, lemon juice and rind, and olive oil in a bowl. Season with salt and pepper to taste. Place a hot salmon fillet on each salad, drizzle the dressing over it, and serve.

NOTES

Summer greens, mozzarella, and basil salad

SERVES 4

2 large handfuls mixed summer greens, such as lollo rosso lettuce, romaine, and corn salad (mâche)
12 oz. cherry tomatoes, cut in half
2 balls mozzarella cheese, torn into bite-size chunks
2 avocados

FOR THE DRESSING

handful of fresh basil leaves
2 tsp. capers, rinsed
1 tsp. Dijon mustard
pinch of sugar
1 tbsp. red wine vinegar
¼ cup olive oil
salt and freshly ground black pepper

First make the dressing. Put the basil, capers, mustard, sugar, vinegar, and oil in a blender and blend until smooth. Season to taste with salt and pepper and set aside. (The capers are already salty, so you may not need to add any extra salt.)

Divide the greens among four individual serving bowls and scatter the tomatoes and mozzarella on top.

Cut the avocados in half, remove the pits, then peel and cut the flesh into bite-size chunks. Scatter it over the salads.

Drizzle the dressing over the top of each serving, toss to combine well, and serve immediately.

Summer greens with lemon and chili squid

SERVES 4

12 oz. squid, cleaned
juice of 2 lemons
pinch of dried red pepper flakes
2 large handfuls mixed summer greens, such as Bibb lettuce, oakleaf, and arugula
1 red bell pepper, chopped
4 tomatoes, cut into eighths
½ English cucumber, sliced
2 tbsp. finely chopped fresh mint leaves
pinch of sugar
½ tsp. grated lemon rind
4 tbsp. olive oil
salt

Prepare the already cleaned squid by separating the tentacles from the body pouch, then cutting both into large bite-size pieces. Put in a bowl, pour in half the lemon juice, sprinkle with the red pepper flakes, and leave to marinate for at least 15 minutes.

Meanwhile, make the salad. Divide the salad greens between four serving plates and scatter the red bell pepper, tomatoes, and cucumber over them. Make a dressing by whisking together the mint, sugar, remaining lemon juice, lemon rind, and 3 tablespoons of the olive oil. Season to taste with salt and set aside.

Drain the squid and pat dry on paper towels. Brush with the remaining oil, then season well with salt. Heat a grill pan or broiler until very hot, then cook the squid on it for about 45 seconds on each side, until the flesh is opaque and tender. Scatter the squid over the salad servings, drizzle with the dressing, and toss to combine. Serve.

watercress

Wild watercress can be seen growing in summer streams, although the vivid green bunches that arrive in the grocery store have been cultivated in special beds with piped running water and are available all year round. (You should avoid gathering and eating wild watercress, as it has usually been infiltrated by liver flukes—parasites that can cause severe damage to the liver, if ingested.)

The robust, peppery flavor of raw watercress is delicious in salads, or it may be shredded and added to cooked dishes at the last minute. Some people, however, find watercress too powerful on its own, and prefer it combined with blander ingredients or used more as a flavoring. The shredded leaves are excellent stirred into creamy mashed potato just before serving, or combined with milder lettuce leaves in a salad, in a similar manner to fresh herbs. Spread savory scones or bagels with thick cream cheese and top with a sprig of watercress, or shred a handful of watercress leaves and sprinkle them over an omelet while it cooks.

Choose watercress with large dark leaves and avoid any that is withered, limp, or slimy. If a recipe calls for only the leaves, simply pluck them off the stems. For salads, part of the stem is often trimmed off, leaving the more tender upper part and juicy leaves.

Watercress soup (opposite)

SERVES 4
2 tbsp. butter
1 onion, chopped
8 oz. potatoes, chopped
3 cups vegetable stock
6 oz. watercress
1 cup milk
¼ cup light cream
salt and freshly ground black pepper

Melt the butter in a pot, then add the onion and fry gently for about 5 minutes until soft. Add the potatoes, pour in the stock, and let simmer for about 15 minutes until the potatoes are tender.

Meanwhile, remove the green leaves from the watercress and roughly chop the stalks. Add the stalks to the pot and cook for about 2 minutes, then stir in the leaves, reserving a few for garnishing, and cook for about 1 minute more.

Pour the contents of the pot into a food processor or blender and blend until smooth. Return to the pot, stir in the milk, and bring to simmering point. Remove from the heat, stir in the cream, and season to taste with salt and pepper. Serve immediately, garnished with the reserved watercress leaves.

NOTES

peas

Juicy bright-green peas, fresh from their pods, are one of the joys of summer. Once they are picked, however, their sugars rapidly turn into starch and, as peas in their pods are so often days old already when they reach the stores, "fresh" peas may be less sweet than those that have been frozen within hours of picking. But when really fresh peas are available, they are truly wonderful. It is well worth growing your own and picking them just before cooking. Also, try the invariably sweet and delicate snow peas and sugar snap peas, both of which are eaten whole, pod and all.

All types of peas should be cooked very briefly by plunging into boiling water—never salted as this will toughen the skin—until just tender. Then quickly drain and toss with butter, seasoning, and—for a really delicious crowning touch—a scattering of chopped fresh mint. Peas are also fabulous in salads: simply refresh them under cold water as soon as they have been drained and toss them in. Try also adding them to thick omelets or tortillas, or to creamy risotto rice, as in the classic Italian *risi e bisi*, or mash and pile them onto garlic-rubbed toast, then top with twists of prosciutto. Summer peas make wonderful refreshing soups, too, and they are frequently used in Indian curries, while sugar snaps and snow peas, with their sugary tang and crispy texture, make a great addition to Asian-style stir-fries.

Baked chili salmon with smashed peas

SERVES 4
4 salmon fillets,
about 6 oz. each, skinned
salt and freshly ground black pepper
juice of 1 lemon
¼ tsp. dried red pepper flakes
2 tbsp. olive oil
4 shallots, chopped
18 oz. shelled fresh
or frozen peas (about 4 cups)
½ cup white wine

Heat the oven to 400°F. Arrange the salmon fillets in a single layer in a baking dish, season with salt, then sprinkle the lemon juice and red pepper flakes over them. Bake in the oven for about 9 minutes, until just cooked through.

Meanwhile, heat the oil in a frying pan, add the shallots and cook over medium heat for about 3 minutes. Add the peas and wine and simmer for about 5 minutes until tender. Using a blender or potato masher, blend to make a coarse mash. Season to taste with salt and pepper and divide between four warm serving plates. Top each serving with a cooked salmon fillet and serve.

NOTES

Summer pea and ham soup

SERVES 4
2 tbsp. olive oil
2 onions, chopped
18 oz. shelled fresh or
frozen peas (about 4 cups)
4¾ cups vegetable stock
6 tbsp. crème fraîche or sour cream
handful of fresh mint, chopped, plus
extra for garnishing
salt and freshly ground black pepper
4 slices prosciutto, cut into
bite-size pieces

Heat the oil in a large pot, add the onions, and fry gently for about 5 minutes, until soft. Add the peas and stock and bring to a boil. Lower the heat and let simmer gently for about 5 minutes.

Let the pea, onion, and stock mixture cool slightly, then pour into a blender or food processor and blend until smooth. Stir in the crème fraîche and chopped mint and season to taste with salt and pepper.

Heat through, then ladle into four warm serving bowls. Sprinkle the ham and the fresh mint garnish over it, and serve.

Sugar snap pea and roast bell pepper salad

SERVES 4
4 red bell peppers
11 oz. sugar snap peas
2 tsp. red wine vinegar
4 tsp. olive oil
handful of fresh mint, roughly
chopped
salt and freshly ground black pepper

Heat the oven to 400°F.

Place the bell peppers on a baking sheet and roast in the oven for about 1 hour, until the skins are wrinkled and well browned. Transfer to a bowl, cover with plastic wrap, and let cool for about 15 minutes.

When the peppers are cool enough to handle, peel off the skins, cut in half, and discard the core and seeds. Slice the flesh into strips, place in a serving bowl, and set aside.

Plunge the sugar snap peas into a pan of boiling water for about 3 minutes, until just tender but still crisp. Drain and refresh under cold running water. Drain again and add to the peppers.

Whisk together the vinegar, olive oil, and mint, then season to taste with salt and pepper. Pour the dressing over the peppers and peas, toss to combine, and serve.

NOTES

Fragrant sugar snap stir-fry with shrimp

SERVES 4

2 tbsp. oyster sauce
2 tsp. soy sauce
1 tsp. sesame oil
1 tsp. brown sugar
2 tbsp. sunflower oil
1 red chili, seeded and chopped
2 cloves garlic, finely chopped
2-inch piece fresh ginger, peeled and grated
1 lb. sugar snap peas or snow peas
18 oz. raw tiger shrimp, peeled and deveined
bunch of scallions, sliced
large handful of fresh basil, torn
rice or noodles, for serving

Put the oyster sauce, soy sauce, sesame oil, and brown sugar in a small bowl and stir until the sugar has dissolved. Set aside.

Heat the sunflower oil in a wok or large frying pan, then add the chili, garlic, and ginger, and stir-fry for about 30 seconds. Toss in the sugar snap peas and stir-fry for another minute.

Add the shrimp and scallions to the wok and stir-fry for about 2 minutes, until the shrimp turn pink.

Pour over the oyster and soy sauce mixture and cook for about 30 seconds more. Serve immediately on a bed of rice or noodles, with the chopped basil sprinkled over the top.

Green peas braised with lettuce and scallions

SERVES 4

2 tbsp. butter
bunch of scallions, sliced diagonally into 1-inch lengths
2 Bibb lettuces, shredded
11 oz. shelled fresh or frozen peas (about 2¼-2½ cups)
4 sprigs of fresh mint
3 tbsp. white wine
salt and freshly ground black pepper

Melt the butter in a pan. Add the scallions and stir over medium heat for about 1 minute. Add the lettuces and peas and stir to coat in the butter.

Add the mint sprigs and wine, stir, then cover tightly and let cook gently over a low heat for about 15 minutes, stirring occasionally, until the lettuces and peas are tender. Season to taste with salt and pepper and serve immediately.

beans

Beans in their various incarnations are one of the great pleasures of the summer table. Sweet, juicy green beans, fresh-tasting pole beans, and earthy fava beans all have their own merits and are wonderfully versatile. Remember, however, to choose the freshest you can find, as their flavor deteriorates very quickly after picking.

Green beans and pole beans are cooked in a similar way. Just trim off the tops and tails—and for pole or runner beans, strip out any coarse strings and slice—and boil or steam until just tender. Then serve, simply tossed in butter and seasoned with black pepper, or make into a salad by refreshing under cold water and tossing with flaked almonds, finely sliced red onion, and a few tablespoons of vinaigrette. Also try them chopped and tossed into soups and pasta or stewed with tomatoes and summer herbs.

Fava beans need to be removed from their pods before cooking and, on all but the very young beans, the thick gray-green skin should also be removed. Fava beans have a starchy texture, making them good for pureeing and blending into soups and dips. Their mild yet pervasive flavor stands out well in rich stews and other cooked dishes, too. They are, however, great when simply boiled or steamed and served as an accompaniment.

three-bean salad with lemon and mint

Make a dressing by whisking together 4 teaspoons of red wine vinegar, 2½ tablespoons of olive oil, the grated rind of ½ lemon, 1 teaspoon of Dijon mustard, a pinch of sugar, and 1½ teaspoons of chopped fresh mint. Then season to taste with salt and freshly ground black pepper and set aside. Bring a large pot of water to the boil, toss in 1½ cups of shelled fava beans, 1½ cups of trimmed green beans, and 1½ cups of trimmed, sliced pole or runner beans. Cook for about 3 minutes until just tender, then drain and refresh under cold water. Drain again and tip into a salad bowl. If you like, crumble 3 strips of cooked bacon over the top, then pour in the dressing and toss to combine well. Let stand for at least 30 minutes before serving.

NOTES

Fava bean puree with seared scallops

SERVES 4

2 tbsp. olive oil

3 shallots, finely chopped

1 lb. shelled fava beans (about 3 cups)

5 tbsp. white wine

salt and freshly ground black pepper

FOR THE SCALLOPS

16-20 scallops, cleaned

½ clove garlic, finely chopped

1 red chili, seeded and finely chopped

juice and grated rind of 1 lime

1 tbsp. olive oil

6 fresh mint leaves, shredded

Heat the oil in a pan. Add the shallots and gently fry over a medium-low heat for about 3 minutes. Add the beans, pour in the wine, cover, and simmer over a low heat for about 6 minutes until tender. Put the beans and juices in a food processor or blender and blend to make a smooth puree. Return to the pan and season to taste with salt and pepper. Set aside and keep warm.

Place the scallops in a large bowl. Whisk together the garlic, chili, and lime juice and zest, season with salt, and pour this over the scallops, turning them to coat well.

Heat the oil in a large frying pan. Add the scallops and cook for 1-2 minutes on each side, until lightly browned and just cooked. Serve immediately with the warm bean puree, spooning over any juices from the pan, and sprinkling with the shredded mint leaves.

Green beans roasted with tomatoes and herb-stuffed trout

SERVES 4

1 lb. green beans, trimmed (about 3-3½ cups)

1 lb. cherry tomatoes (about 3 cups)

2 cloves garlic, thinly sliced

2 tbsp. olive oil

salt and freshly ground black pepper

4 trout, about 14 oz. each, cleaned

1½ lemons

bunch of fresh thyme

Heat the oven to 425°F. Put the beans and tomatoes in a large baking dish or roasting pan and sprinkle the garlic over them. Drizzle with the oil, season with salt and pepper, and toss to coat well.

Make several slashes in the skin of each trout, then season all over with salt and pepper. Slice one of the lemons and stuff into the cavity of each fish with some sprigs of thyme, then squeeze a little juice from the lemon half over each fish.

Nestle the prepared fish in among the beans and tomatoes in the baking dish. Cook in the oven for about 15 minutes, until the trout are cooked through and the beans and tomatoes are tender. Serve.

NOTES

okra

The okra plant is native to Africa and its long, ridged seed pods are widely used in the cooking of that continent, as well as in the cuisines of the Caribbean, India, and the Mediterranean. Okra is usually stewed, although it may be fried or steamed before combining with other ingredients.

The seeds are coated in a slimy substance that is released into dishes containing chopped or sliced okra, giving them a somewhat gloopy consistency. This is relished by some and is often exploited as a deliberate characteristic of okra dishes. But if it is not to your taste, okra pods can simply be trimmed and cooked whole, so that the viscous liquid cannot ooze out. The end result will still capture the delicate but distinct flavor of okra and is truly delicious.

When buying, look for small, bright-green pods that are firm and slightly springy when squeezed. To prepare them, trim off the stem without revealing the seeds, then either leave whole or cut up as called for in the recipe.

Mediterranean okra and tomato stew

This simple Mediterranean-style dish, mildly spiced with coriander seed, is the perfect way to enjoy tender whole okra. Serve it hot, warm, or at room temperature—as a vegetable accompaniment or as an appetizer, with chunks of crusty bread for mopping up the juices.

SERVES 4
2 tbsp. olive oil
1 onion, cut in half and sliced
2 cloves garlic, finely chopped
2 tsp. ground coriander seed
1¼ lb. ripe tomatoes, peeled, seeded, and chopped (about 2½ cups)
½ cup white wine
¼ cup water
salt and freshly ground black pepper
1 lb. okra, trimmed
large handful of fresh flat-leaf parsley, chopped

Heat the oil in a large pan. Add the onion and garlic and gently fry for about 5 minutes. Stir in the coriander seed, then add the tomatoes, wine, and water. Season to taste with salt and pepper, and stir. Add the okra and gently fold in.

Bring to a boil, reduce the heat, cover, and let simmer gently for about 20 minutes, stirring occasionally, until the okra is tender. Check the seasoning and serve, with the chopped parsley sprinkled over the top.

NOTES

Chicken and okra gumbo

This spicy soupy stew is a classic of the Cajun kitchen. Here, the okra is sliced to release its viscous juices, giving the gumbo its distinctive, thick consistency.

SERVES 4

2 tbsp. olive oil
1 onion, chopped
2 cloves garlic, finely chopped
1½ tbsp. all-purpose flour
2¼ cups chicken stock
2 green bell peppers, chopped
9 oz. okra, trimmed and cut into
½-inch slices (about 2½ cups)
3 tomatoes, peeled, seeded,
and chopped
2 tbsp. tomato paste
leaves from 3-4 sprigs of
fresh thyme
1 tsp. cayenne pepper
11oz. cooked chicken, cut into bite-
size pieces
1 cup corn kernels
Tabasco sauce, to taste
rice, for serving

Heat the oil in a large pan. Add the onion and garlic and fry gently for about 5 minutes. Stir in the flour and cook for another minute.

Remove from the heat, gradually stir in the chicken stock, then add the green bell peppers, okra, tomatoes, tomato paste, thyme leaves, and cayenne pepper. Bring to a boil, reduce the heat, cover, and let simmer for about 45 minutes, stirring occasionally to stop the gumbo from sticking to the bottom of the pan.

Stir in the chicken and corn and cook for 30 minutes more, stirring occasionally. Add Tabasco sauce to taste. Serve in the traditional manner—ladled over rice.

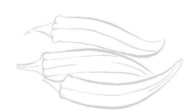

indian-spiced okra

In India, okra—often referred to as "ladies' fingers"—is a popular vegetable accompaniment. To prepare in the Indian manner, heat about 2 tablespoons of oil in a large pan, then add 2 chopped onions and fry gently for about 5 minutes. Toss in 2 crushed garlic cloves and a few teaspoons of grated fresh ginger and fry for another 2 minutes, stirring. Then stir in ½ teaspoon each of chili powder and ground turmeric, and 1½ teaspoons each of ground coriander seed and ground cumin, followed by 4 tomatoes that have been peeled, seeded, and chopped. Add 11 ounces of trimmed okra, season to taste with salt, cover, and cook over a gentle heat for about 20 minutes, stirring from time to time, until the okra is tender. Check the seasoning and serve sprinkled with chopped fresh cilantro or mint.

broccoli

The name broccoli comes from the Italian word for "arm" or "shoot," which is a wonderful description of the appearance of the tiny unopened flowerheads clustered at the end of broccoli's fleshy stems. A member of the cabbage family, broccoli for some reason seems infinitely more sophisticated a vegetable than cabbage and has a milder flavor. The most commonly found broccoli is calabrese, with its fat, round, bluish-green heads. It is in season from summer into early autumn. The exotic-looking broccoli romanesco, with its elegant, pointed, lime-green heads—which would not look out of place in a bouquet of flowers—follows later.

Despite its many incarnations, the different varieties of broccoli taste very similar and can be cooked in the same way—steamed or boiled as a simple accompaniment, added to stir-fries, pies and tarts, and salads, tossed with pasta or cooked in gratins. Frequently paired with cauliflower, broccoli also goes well with cheese and hollandaise sauces and chopped bacon.

The heads are often regarded as the main attraction when it comes to eating broccoli, but the juicy stems are as much of a pleasure, so do not just cut them off and discard them. As stems are usually covered in a thick coarse skin, it is a good idea to peel this off before cooking.

When buying, look for fresh, green specimens and avoid any that have soft or withered stems, yellowing heads, or heads speckled with dark patches or spots. To prepare, wash well, break the heads into florets, and peel and cut the stems into bite-size pieces. Then boil, steam, or stir-fry until just tender. Avoid overcooking.

stir-fried broccoli with ginger and garlic

Fresh, bright-green broccoli is perfect for stir-frying. Cut the stems and florets into bite-size pieces and set aside. Heat 2 tablespoons of sunflower oil in a wok, then toss in 2 crushed garlic cloves and about 2 teaspoons of grated fresh ginger and stir-fry for about 30 seconds. Add the prepared broccoli, followed by a pinch of dried red pepper flakes, then toss it over the heat for about 2 minutes. Sprinkle in 1–2 teaspoons of soy sauce and 1½ teaspoons of mirin, and toss for another minute. Serve immediately.

NOTES

Orecchiette with broccoli and anchovies

Traditionally, orecchiette—or "little ears"—are used in this southern Italian dish, but any short pasta such as penne (mostaccioli) or bow ties can be substituted.

SERVES 4

11 oz. orecchiette or other short pasta (about 4 cups)
salt and freshly ground black pepper
2 lb. broccoli, heads cut into florets and stems peeled and sliced
2 tbsp. olive oil
1 onion, finely chopped
3 cloves garlic, finely chopped
2-oz. can anchovies, drained and finely chopped
½ cup grated Parmesan cheese

Cook the pasta in a large pot of boiling salted water, according to the instructions on the package.

While the pasta is cooking, cook the broccoli in a separate pot of boiling salted water for about 5 minutes, or until just tender. Drain, reserving a little of the cooking water.

Heat the oil in another large pan, add the onion and garlic, and fry gently for about 5 minutes, until soft. Add the broccoli and about ¼ cup of the reserved cooking water and gently crush the broccoli florets with the back of a spoon. Stir in the anchovies, crushing them into the mixture, and season to taste with black pepper.

Toss the cooked pasta with the broccoli and anchovy mixture. Serve immediately, sprinkled with the Parmesan.

Broccoli and blue cheese tart with walnut crust

SERVES 6

⅔ cup all-purpose flour
½ cup walnuts, chopped
salt and freshly ground black pepper
3 tbsp. butter, chilled and cut up
about 1 tbsp. cold water
11 oz. broccoli, heads cut into florets and stems peeled and sliced
2 tbsp. olive oil
1 onion, finely chopped
4 eggs
6 tbsp. crème fraîche or sour cream
⅔ cup cubed Gorgonzola or other blue cheese

Put the flour, walnuts, and a pinch of salt in a food processor and blend until the nuts are ground. Add the butter and blend until the mixture resembles fine bread crumbs. With the machine running, add just enough water for the mixture to come together to form a soft ball of dough. Wrap in plastic wrap and chill in the fridge for 30 minutes.

Meanwhile, steam the broccoli for 5 minutes, until just tender, then set aside. Heat the oil in a large pan, add the onion, and cook for about 5 minutes. Toss in the broccoli, crush lightly with the back of a spoon, then set aside. Heat the oven to 400°F.

Roll out the dough to line an 8-inch tart pan. Cover with foil, scatter in some baking beans, and bake in the oven for 10 minutes. Remove the foil and beans and cook for 5-10 minutes more until the bottom is crisp. Beat together the eggs and crème fraîche in a bowl, season well with salt and pepper, then set aside.

Scatter the cheese over the bottom of the pie shell, top with the broccoli, then pour in the egg mixture. Bake for about 20 minutes, until the filling is just set and golden. Serve warm or cold.

bell peppers

An assortment of different bell peppers is available throughout the summer and well into the fll. Most are either green, red, orange, or yellow in color, though they do come in other hues, including the more unusual purple-black variety. They range in shape from squat and round to long and tapered and they vary in flavor, too. Green bell peppers are in fact the same as red ones, but are picked before ripening, giving them a sharper, more savory tang. Red bell peppers, along with the orange and yellow varieties, have a marked sweetness. Black peppers have a similar flavor to green ones and, since they turn green upon cooking, are best used raw.

Crisp and juicy, raw peppers are delicious in salads. When cooked, they become succulent and tender and the sweeter-flavored peppers become even sweeter. They can be broiled or grilled, roasted, sautéed, stewed, and stuffed. They are a staple of Mediterranean cuisine—added to countless appetizers, sauces, and stews, made into soup, scattered on pizzas, and tossed with pasta.

Buy only peppers that are firm and glossy. Avoid any that are soft, wrinkled, or blemished. Bell peppers are usually seeded before cooking. To do this, cut in half through the stem and gently pull the two sides apart, then strip away the seeds and pithy membrane, before chopping or slicing for your recipe. To seed and prepare for stuffing whole, just cut around the stalk and gently wiggle and pull it out along with the core and seeds. Any loose seeds can then be shaken out and the white pith inside trimmed away using a long-bladed knife.

roast bell peppers

Roasting sweet red, yellow, or orange bell peppers until blackened all over intensifies their sweetness and depth of flavor and gives them a luscious soft texture.

Place the bell peppers on a baking sheet, then bake in an oven heated to 450°F until blackened. Transfer to a bowl and cover with plastic wrap, then let stand for about 10 minutes.

When the peppers are cool enough to handle, peel off the skin and remove the stalk and seeds, then use the peppers as your recipe calls for. Don't rinse the peppers after roasting, as they will lose their intense, caramely, smoky flavor.

NOTES

Roast bell pepper, tomato, and mozzarella salad

SERVES 4

6 ripe medium tomatoes
8 canned anchovy fillets, drained
and cut in half lengthwise
2 red bell peppers, roasted (see
page 86), peeled, and seeded
2 yellow bell peppers, roasted (see
page 86), peeled, and seeded
2 balls of mozzarella cheese, about
9 oz. in total
2 handfuls of fresh basil leaves
2 tbsp. capers, rinsed and chopped
1 clove garlic, crushed
1 tbsp. red wine vinegar
4 tbsp. olive oil
freshly ground black pepper
crusty French bread, for serving

Cut a cross in the skin on the bottom of each tomato, place in a heatproof bowl, and pour in boiling water to cover. Let stand for about 30 seconds, then drain and peel. Cut the tomatoes in half, remove the tough core, and scoop the seeds into a strainer placed over a bowl. Press the seeds with the back of a spoon to squeeze out the juice, then discard the seeds and reserve the juice.

Chop the tomatoes into bite-size pieces and place in a salad bowl with the anchovies. Cut the bell peppers and mozzarella into bite-size pieces and add to the tomatoes. Tear the basil leaves and scatter them over the top.

Add the capers, garlic, vinegar, and oil, and a good grinding of black pepper to the reserved tomato juice and whisk together. Pour it over the salad, toss to combine, then let stand for about 15 minutes. Serve with plenty of bread for mopping up the juices.

Lamb steaks with sweet bell pepper relish

SERVES 4

4 lamb leg steaks, about
7 oz. each
2 cloves garlic, finely chopped
2 tsp. ground cumin
1 tsp. paprika
juice of 1 lemon
3 tbsp. olive oil
salt and freshly ground black pepper
2 red bell peppers, seeded and
roughly chopped
1 tsp. balsamic vinegar
2 tsp. capers, rinsed
handful of fresh basil leaves

Place the lamb steaks in a large dish. Whisk together half the garlic with the cumin, paprika, lemon juice, and 1 tablespoon of the olive oil, then season to taste with salt and pepper. Pour it over the steaks, turning to coat, then cover and let marinate in the fridge for 1 hour.

To prepare the relish, heat the remaining oil in a frying pan. Add the remaining garlic and fry gently for about 1 minute. Add the red peppers and cook, stirring frequently, for about 20 minutes, until tender. Tip into a food processor or blender, add the vinegar and capers, and blend until smooth. Add the basil, pulse briefly to chop, then season to taste with salt and pepper. Set aside.

Heat the broiler to hot and cook the leg steaks under it for about 6 minutes on each side, or until cooked to your liking. Serve immediately with the warm relish.

Pepperonata pizza with summer vegetables (opposite)

This recipe makes two large pizzas, though, if you prefer, you can divide the dough into four pieces to make four smaller ones. The sweet red and yellow bell pepper sauce makes a wonderful base for the tender, juicy, charbroiled vegetables and melting mozzarella.

MAKES 2 LARGE PIZZAS

3 cups white bread flour
2 x ¼-oz. (7 g) envelopes of rapid-rise (fast-action) dried yeast
1 tsp. salt
1 cup lukewarm water
2 tbsp. olive oil, plus extra for brushing
2 cloves garlic, chopped
1 red bell pepper, seeded and cut lengthwise into strips
1 yellow bell pepper, seeded and cut lengthwise into strips
1 cup tomato puree
salt and freshly ground black pepper
handful of fresh basil leaves
1 zucchini, cut into round slices
1 small eggplant, cut into round slices
2 balls of mozzarella cheese, about 5 oz. each, cut up
handful of black olives (optional)

Combine the flour, yeast, and salt in a large bowl and make a well in the center. Pour the water into the well and gradually work the flour mixture into it to make a soft, non-sticky dough. Turn out on to a lightly floured surface and knead for 5–10 minutes until the dough becomes smooth and elastic. Place in a lightly oiled bowl, cover in plastic wrap and let rise in a warm place for about 45 minutes, until doubled in size.

Meanwhile, prepare the pepperonata sauce and charbroiled vegetables. Heat the oil in a large pan, add the garlic, and fry gently for about 2 minutes, then add the bell peppers and cook gently for another 5 minutes. Add the tomato puree, season to taste with salt and pepper, cover, and simmer for about 25 minutes, stirring occasionally, particularly towards the end of the cooking time. Remove from the heat, tear half the basil leaves into the sauce, check the seasoning, then set aside.

While the sauce is simmering, heat the oven to 425°C. Heat a ridged grill pan or broiler until hot. Brush the eggplant and zucchini slices on both sides with a little olive oil and season with salt and pepper, then, working in batches, cook on the hot grill pan or under the broiler for about 3 minutes on each side until charred and tender. Set aside.

On a lightly floured surface, punch down the dough and divide into two pieces. Press each one flat and roll out to form two round 10-inch pizzas.

Spread the pepperonata sauce over the pizzas and arrange the cooked vegetables and mozzarella on top. Scatter over the olives on top, if using, and bake in the oven for 15-20 minutes, until the cheese is bubbling and the crust golden. Grind some black pepper over it, sprinkle with the remaining basil leaves, and serve.

NOTES

tomatoes

Ripened in the hot summer sunshine, tomatoes should be juicy, sweet, and intensely flavored and equally good whether they are eaten raw or cooked. In season well into the fall, they are used around the world as a base for sauces, stews, soups, and salads. They can even be made into ice creams and sherbets. They come in a fabulous array of shapes, sizes, and colors—round or plum-shaped, smooth or ridged, huge or tiny, and in various shades of red, orange, yellow, or green.

When buying tomatoes, choose those that are deeply colored and unblemished. They take little preparation, although some recipes may call for them to be peeled and seeded. To peel, cut a cross in the skin on the bottom of each tomato and place in a heatproof bowl. Pour in boiling water to cover and let stand for about 30 seconds, then drain. The skins should peel away easily. To remove the seeds, slice in half, cut out the core, and gently press out the seeds with your thumb. A fragrant sauce can be made by gently frying 2 crushed garlic cloves in 2 tablespoons of olive oil for 1-2 minutes, then adding 1½ pounds of tomatoes that have been peeled, seeded, and chopped. Simmer gently for about 15 minutes and season to taste with salt and freshly ground black pepper. Remove from the heat, stir in a handful of torn fresh basil leaves, and use.

Oven-dried tomatoes on garlic bruschetta

MAKES 12
1 lb. cherry tomatoes, cut in half
(about 3 cups)
2 cloves garlic, finely chopped
3 tbsp. olive oil
salt and freshly ground black pepper

FOR THE BRUSCHETTA
12 slices baguette or ciabatta,
¾-inch thick
1 clove garlic, cut in half
handful of fresh basil leaves
extra virgin olive oil, for drizzling

Heat the oven to 325°F. Arrange the tomatoes, cut-side up, in a baking dish. Mix the garlic and olive oil in a small bowl, season to taste with salt and pepper, and spoon the mixture over the tomatoes. Bake in the oven for 1-1¼ hours, until the tomatoes are slightly shriveled but still red. Remove from the oven and let cool.

To make the bruschetta, broil the bread on both sides until golden, then rub one side of each slice with the cut garlic clove. Top with tomato halves, spooning over them any juices, add a couple of basil leaves, then drizzle with oil and serve.

NOTES

Gazpacho

SERVES 4

2 lb. ripe tomatoes, peeled (see page 90), seeded, and chopped
½ English cucumber, peeled and chopped
1 red bell pepper, seeded and chopped
2 cloves garlic, chopped
2 tbsp. sherry vinegar or red wine vinegar
4 tbsp. olive oil
3 slices white bread, crusts removed
1⅔ cups cold water
salt and freshly ground black pepper
croûtons and fresh basil leaves, for serving

Put the tomatoes, cucumber, red bell pepper, garlic, vinegar, and olive oil in a blender or food processor. Tear up the bread into small chunks and sprinkle it in, then pour in about half the water. Blend to make a smooth puree.

Pour the puree into a large bowl, stir in the remaining water and season to taste with salt and pepper. Cover and let chill in the fridge for at least 2 hours.

Serve with croûtons and roughly torn fresh basil leaves sprinkled over each serving.

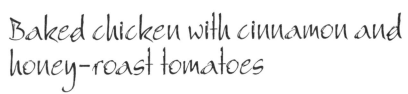

Baked chicken with cinnamon and honey-roast tomatoes

SERVES 4

4 skinless chicken breasts, about 7 oz. each
1 clove garlic, crushed
1 tsp. smoked paprika
juice of 1 lemon
2 tbsp. olive oil
salt and freshly ground black pepper
8 ripe medium tomatoes, cut in half
1 tsp. ground cinnamon
2-3 tsp. honey

Arrange the chicken breasts in a single layer in a baking dish. In a small bowl, whisk together the garlic, paprika, lemon juice, and half the olive oil. Season to taste with salt and pepper, then pour over the chicken breasts and turn to coat well. Cover and let marinate in the fridge for at least 1 hour.

Heat the oven to 425°F. Tuck in the tomatoes, cut-side up, around the chicken breasts. Sprinkle the cinnamon over them, season well with salt and pepper, then drizzle the honey and the remaining olive oil on top.

Bake in the oven for about 25 minutes, spooning the juices over them once or twice during the cooking time, until the tomatoes are tender and the chicken cooked through. Serve.

Tomato, red bell pepper, and ricotta tartlets

SERVES 4

2 large red bell peppers, roasted
(see page 86), peeled, and seeded
6₂ oz. cherry tomatoes (about 1 cup)
1 tsp. balsamic vinegar
4 oz. ricotta cheese (about ½ cup)
salt and freshly ground black pepper
olive oil, for drizzling
few fresh basil leaves, for serving

FOR THE DOUGH

⅓ cup walnuts
¾ cup whole-wheat flour
pinch of salt
¼ cup (½ stick) butter, chilled and
cut up
about 1 tbsp. cold water

First make the dough. Put the walnuts in a food processor and blend until ground. Add the flour and salt and pulse to combine. Add the butter and blend until the mixture resembles fine bread crumbs. With the motor running, gradually add just enough cold water for the mixture to come together and form a ball. Wrap in plastic wrap and chill in the fridge for about 30 minutes.

Heat the oven to 375°F. Roll out the dough and line four greased 4-inch tartlet molds with it. Cover each with foil, fill with baking beans, and bake in the oven for 8 minutes. Remove the foil and beans, then bake for 4 minutes more until the bases are dry. Remove from the oven and reduce the temperature to 350°F.

Meanwhile, cut the bell peppers into strips and cut the tomatoes in half. Divide the pepper strips between the baked pie shells, then tuck the tomatoes in among them. Drizzle with balsamic vinegar and top with a large spoonful of ricotta. Season to taste with salt and pepper and bake in the oven for about 20 minutes. Serve hot or cold, drizzled with olive oil and scattered with fresh basil.

Meatballs in tomato sauce

SERVES 4

12 oz. ground lean beef (about
1½ cups)
1 onion, grated
1 clove garlic, crushed
2 tsp. finely chopped fresh thyme
2 tbsp. grated Parmesan cheese
salt and freshly ground black pepper
1 tbsp. olive oil
1 lb. tomatoes, peeled (see page 90),
seeded, and chopped
6 sun-dried tomatoes in oil, drained
and sliced
spaghetti, for serving

In a large bowl, combine the beef, onion, garlic, half the thyme, and the Parmesan cheese, and season well with salt and pepper. Roll the mixture into 35–40 bite-size balls. Place on a plate, cover, and let chill in the fridge for at least 30 minutes.

Heat the oil in a large frying pan until hot, then add the meatballs and cook over medium-high heat until they are browned all over. Work in batches if necessary.

If you worked in batches, return all the meatballs to the pan. Add the fresh and sun-dried tomatoes and the remaining thyme, season to taste with salt and pepper, lower the heat, and let simmer gently for about 20 minutes, until the meatballs are cooked through and tender. Serve with spaghetti.

NOTES

eggplants

A central ingredient in the Mediterranean kitchen, the eggplant is actually a native of Asia and holds a prominent place in that continent's cuisine as well. In season from midsummer and into the fall, they thrive in warm, sunny climates, although they can be grown in cooler regions too. There are many different varieties, coming in a vast array of shapes, sizes, and colors. Plump, glossy, purple-black eggplants may be large or small enough to be eaten in two or three mouthfuls. Then there are the lavender-purple, green, and creamy-white varieties, some long and thin, others fat and round or small and egg-shaped. And, in addition, there are also the tiny hard pea eggplants (*makua phuong*), barely the size of a large pea, that are frequently used in Thai curries and that explode tantalizingly in your mouth as you bite into them.

Eggplants are delicious stewed in dishes such as French *ratatouille* and Indian and Thai curries, baked as in Greek *moussaka* and Italian-American *parmigiana di melanzane,* or simply sliced, dipped in batter, and deep-fried. They become tender and juicy with an almost meaty texture when cooked and readily absorb the flavors of the other ingredients they are with.

When buying, look for firm, shiny specimens and avoid any that are soft or wrinkled. Size makes little difference to flavor and texture, so choose eggplants that are appropriate to the recipe. The larger ones, for example, are great for stuffing and the smallest ones are ideal for using whole in curries and stew.

simple eggplant dip

The soft flesh of baked eggplants is used throughout the Mediterranean and Middle East to make a delicious dip for serving as an appetizer, a side dish, or part of a *mezze.* Simply take 2 large eggplants, prick them with a fork and bake in a heated oven at 400°F for about 30-40 minutes, until soft. Scoop out the creamy flesh into a blender or food processor and discard the skins. Add 2 chopped garlic cloves, ½ a sliced onion, the juice of 1 lemon, and a handful of roughly chopped fresh flat-leaf parsley. Blend until smooth. Season to taste with salt and freshly ground black pepper and serve with more chopped parsley sprinkled over it.

NOTES

Melting eggplant and Parmesan rolls

In this twist on the classic *parmigiana di melanzane*, the eggplants are sliced lengthwise and rolled around tomatoes and melting mozzarella.

SERVES 4

2 tbsp. olive oil, plus extra
for brushing
2 cloves garlic, finely chopped
1½ lb. ripe tomatoes, peeled (see
page 90) and coarsely chopped
(about 2½–3 cups)
salt and freshly ground black pepper
large handful of fresh basil leaves
2 eggplants, cut lengthwise into
⅛-inch thick slices
1 ball of mozzarella cheese,
about 6 oz., cut up
1 cup grated Parmesan cheese

Heat the oven to 400°F. Grease a large baking dish thoroughly.

Heat the oil in a pan, add the garlic, and fry gently for 1–2 minutes. Add the tomatoes, season with salt and pepper, lower the heat, and let simmer for about 15 minutes, until you have a thick sauce. Remove from the heat, tear half the basil leaves into the sauce, check the seasoning, and set aside.

Meanwhile, heat a ridged grill pan or broiler until hot. Brush the eggplant slices lightly with oil on both sides. Season with salt and pepper and, working in batches, cook on the grill pan or under the broiler for about 3 minutes on each side, until charred and tender. Roll them up and keep the cooked slices warm while cooking the rest.

Unroll the eggplant slices, drizzle a spoonful of tomato sauce in the center of each one, sprinkle in a few cubes of mozzarella and a little Parmesan, then top with a little more sauce. Roll up and place in the baking dish, folded side down. Sprinkle the remaining Parmesan over them, add a grinding of black pepper, and bake in the oven for about 15 minutes until tender and golden. Serve sprinkled with the remaining basil leaves.

Warm eggplant salad with herb salsa (opposite)

SERVES 4

½ clove garlic

large handful of fresh basil leaves, plus extra for garnishing

5 tbsp. olive oil, plus extra for brushing

1 tbsp. balsamic vinegar

2 tbsp. capers, rinsed

salt and freshly ground black pepper

1 tbsp. pine nuts

2 large eggplants

Make a dressing by putting the garlic, basil, olive oil, vinegar, and capers in a food processor or blender. Blend until smooth, season to taste with salt and pepper, and set aside.

Heat a dry frying pan, add the pine nuts and toss over the heat for about 3 minutes until golden and toasted. Remove from the pan and set aside.

Slice the eggplants lengthwise into ¼-inch-thick slices and brush on both sides with olive oil, then season with salt and pepper. Heat a ridged grill pan or broiler until hot, then, working in batches, cook the eggplant slices in the pan or under the broiler for about 3 minutes on each side, until charred and tender. Roll up and keep the cooked slices warm while cooking the rest.

Divide the cooked eggplant slices among four serving plates, drizzle the dressing over them, sprinkle the toasted pine nuts on top, and serve, scattered with a few fresh basil leaves.

Sicilian eggplant salad

SERVES 4

3 tbsp. olive oil

2 cloves garlic, thinly sliced

1 onion, cut in half and thinly sliced

1 eggplant, cut into ½-inch cubes

1 tbsp. tomato paste

½ cup vegetable stock

3 ripe tomatoes, peeled (see page 90) and chopped

1 tsp. red wine vinegar

2 tsp. sugar

2 tbsp. capers, rinsed

handful of green olives, pitted

freshly ground black pepper

large handful of fresh flat-leaf parsley, roughly chopped

Heat the oil in a large frying pan, add the garlic and onion, and gently fry for about 5 minutes. Toss in the eggplant and cook for another 10 minutes, stirring occasionally.

Blend the tomato paste and stock together in a clean pan, then add to the eggplants with the tomatoes, vinegar, sugar, capers, and olives, and season to taste with black pepper. Bring to a boil, then lower the heat and let simmer for about 15 minutes, stirring occasionally, until the eggplant is tender. Check the seasoning and adjust if necessary.

Transfer to a bowl and let stand for at least 30 minutes. Serve at room temperature, sprinkled with the chopped parsley.

NOTES

cucumbers

Made up almost entirely of water, the juicy, refreshing cucumber comes in many shapes and sizes, from tiny, knobbly specimens to long, plump, smooth-skinned ones—and, although they are subtle, there are distinct shifts of flavor between the different varieties.

Cucumbers are used all over the world, especially in salads and relishes, their mild flavor often being used to carry stronger flavorings or to provide a calming accompaniment to fiercer seasonings, such as chilies and spices. They are frequently paired with yogurt, sour cream, and cheese—a tradition that spreads from the eastern Mediterranean right through the Middle East and into India. Chopped cucumber is a central ingredient of *raita*, a cooling, minty yogurt relish for serving alongside spicy curries, while in Greece it is stirred with yogurt and mint to make the dip *tzatziki*, and the similar *cacik* in Turkey and other parts of the Middle East. It is also popular pickled or marinated with herbs, vinegar, and spices—a tradition particularly associated with Central and Eastern Europe.

When buying, look for firm cucumbers. Although the skin is edible, it can easily be removed using a vegetable peeler, if you like. You can also quickly remove the seeds by cutting the cucumber in half lengthwise and scooping them out with a teaspoon. The flesh may then be sliced, chopped, grated, or cut into sticks, ready to add to any dish you choose.

tzatziki

Peel, seed, and grate 1 small or ½ a large cucumber into a strainer and press out as much liquid as possible. Tip the remaining flesh into a bowl and combine with 1 cup of Greek yogurt (or whole-milk), 1 crushed clove garlic, and 2 tablespoons of chopped fresh mint. Stir in salt to taste, then chill in the fridge until ready to serve.

NOTES

Cucumber and mango salad

Crunchy, refreshing cucumber is perfect for adding to any summer salad. Its mild taste and crispness provide a great foundation upon which to build other flavors, textures and colors to create a really zingy and interesting dish. The juicy summer fruits used here are excellent combined with the crisp vegetables—their sweetness offsetting and enhancing both the flavor of the vegetables and the tartness of the vinegar. Although the recipe given below uses mangoes or peaches, other seasonal fruits can be substituted, according to availability. Good alternatives might include a few of handfuls of blueberries or strawberries, or perhaps some pitted cherries. But whatever fruit you decide to use, always make sure that it is really ripe and bursting with flavor.

SERVES 4

1 cucumber, seeded and chopped
1 tomato, seeded and chopped
2 green bell peppers, seeded and chopped
2 small mangoes or 2 large peaches, pitted, peeled, and chopped
salt and freshly ground black pepper
1½ tbsp. red wine vinegar
2 tbsp. olive oil

Put the cucumber, tomato, green bell peppers, and mangoes or peaches in a large serving bowl and season to taste with salt and pepper.

Whisk together the red wine vinegar and olive oil in a small bowl to make a simple dressing. Drizzle this over the vegetables and fruit, toss to combine thoroughly, and serve.

marinated cucumber

This simple sweet-and-sour dish, scented with fragrant dill, makes a good accompaniment to cold meats and broiled fish.

Thinly slice a large cucumber into a colander, sprinkle with a generous pinch of salt, tossing to coat, then let drain for about 30 minutes. Meanwhile, heat a dry frying pan, add 1 teaspoon of coriander seed, and toast them. Place in a mortar, lightly crush them, then combine with 2 tablespoons of white wine vinegar and 1 teaspoon of sugar. Squeeze out as much liquid from the cucumber as possible, place in a bowl, sprinkle with a large handful of finely chopped fresh dill, and pour in the vinegar mixture. Toss to coat and chill for at least 1 hour before serving.

NOTES

summer squashes

Available from midsummer and through into the fall, summer squashes—usually distinguishable from the winter varieties by their thin edible skin—come in a wide range of shapes and sizes, often with skins in vibrant eye-catching hues of green, yellow, or orange. Dark-green zucchinis and bright-yellow, bulb-bottomed crooknecks with their curved stems are probably the most readily available, but the tiny fying-saucer-shaped pattypans are also part of the same family, and well worth looking out for. In England, the enormous zucchinis known as marrows can grow to a massive size, but are best eaten when still fairly small.

All summer squashes are delicately flavored and have tender juicy flesh when cooked. Really small and tender zucchinis, pattypans, and crookneck squashes can be cooked whole, if you like, then simply tossed in butter and seasoned, but larger squashes should be topped and tailed, then sliced, chopped, or grated before using. They may be boiled, sautéed, or broiled. Zucchinis, crookneck squashes, and pattypans are all delicious served hot or cold in salads, pasta dishes, and tarts, and also make a good addition to summer vegetable stews and sauces.

When buying summer squashes, remember to select only the firm, glossy specimens. Avoid any that are limp and dull-looking or have soft patches.

deep-fried zucchini flowers

Zucchini flowers are available in late spring and early summer. They can be added to salads and pasta dishes and make a delicious appetizer when deep-fried. To prepare, whisk together ¾ cup of flour, ⅔ cup of light Italian (or other) beer, and a pinch of salt to make a smooth batter. In a separate bowl, whisk 1 egg white until stiff, then fold it into the batter. Fill a large pan about two-thirds full with vegetable oil and heat until just starting to smoke (about 375ºF). Working in batches of 4–5 flowerheads at a time, dip them in the batter, then drop into the hot oil and cook for 2–3 minutes until crisp and golden. Lift out using a slotted spoon and drain on paper towels. Serve, sprinkled with salt.

NOTES

Charbroiled zucchini and feta salad

SERVES 4

2 tbsp. chopped fresh mint leaves
juice and grated rind of ½ lemon
pinch of sugar
3 tbsp. olive oil, plus extra for
brushing
salt and freshly ground black pepper
4 zucchinis, cut diagonally into
¼-inch thick slices
6 oz. feta cheese (about 1½ cups)

Make a dressing by putting the mint, lemon juice and rind, sugar and olive oil in a bowl and seasoning with a little salt and plenty of pepper. Whisk until well blended, then set aside.

Brush the zucchini slices with a little oil. Heat a grill pan or broiler until hot and cook the zucchinis for about 2-3 minutes on each side, until just tender. (You will probably need to work in batches.)

Put the hot zucchinis in a large serving bowl, crumble the feta cheese over it, pour in the dressing, toss to combine, and serve either warm or at room temperature.

Spaghetti with zucchinis and capers

SERVES 4

2 tbsp. olive oil
1 onion, finely chopped
2 cloves garlic, finely chopped
4 zucchinis, grated
1 tbsp. capers, rinsed and chopped,
plus 1½ tbsp. whole capers, rinsed
11 oz. spaghetti
salt and freshly ground black pepper
1½ cups grated Parmesan cheese

Heat the olive oil in a large pan. Add the onion and garlic and fry gently for about 5 minutes, then add the zucchinis and chopped capers and cook, stirring, for about 10 minutes until the zucchinis are tender. Leave in the pan and set aside.

Meanwhile, cook the pasta in boiling salted water according to the instructions on the package. Drain well.

Stir the whole capers into the zucchini mixture and season well with black pepper and a little salt if necessary. (The capers are salty, so you probably will not need to add any extra salt.) Add the spaghetti and toss to coat, then sprinkle two thirds of the Parmesan cheese over it and toss again. Serve, sprinkled with the remaining cheese.

NOTES

Summer vegetable and tuna kabobs

SERVES 4

1½ cloves garlic, crushed
¼ tsp. roughly chopped fresh
oregano leaves
3 tbsp. olive oil
salt and freshly ground black pepper
1 red onion, seeded and cut
into eighths
2 zucchinis, sliced
1 lb. cherry tomatoes (about 3 cups)
1 red bell pepper, seeded and cut
into chunks
1¼ lb. fresh tuna, cubed

Heat the broiler to hot or prepare the barbecue.

In a small bowl, make a marinade by whisking together the garlic, oregano, and olive oil. Season well with salt and pepper and set aside.

Thread alternate pieces of vegetables and fish onto 12 kabob skewers. Lay in a single layer in a large dish and pour the marinade over them, turning to coat well.

Cook the kabobs under the broiler or on the barbecue for about 8 minutes, until the vegetables are just tender and the fish cooked through, turning the skewers during cooking.

Spiced marrow (large zucchini)

With its mild, juicy flavor, marrow goes well with pungent Indian spices, making a light yet zesty dish. Serve as a vegetable accompaniment or as part of a meal with a varied selection of curries, accompanied by fragrant pilaf rice and flatbreads.

SERVES 4

2 tbsp. tomato paste
1 cup water
2 tbsp. sunflower oil
I onion, cut in half and sliced
2 cloves garlic, sliced
2 green chilies, seeded and sliced
2-inch piece fresh ginger, peeled
and grated
1 tsp. ground coriander seed
½ tsp. turmeric
1 small marrow (or large zucchini),
peeled, seeded, and cut into chunks
salt
juice of ½ lemon
large handful of fresh cilantro,
roughly chopped

Blend the tomato paste with about a quarter of the water in a small bowl, then set aside. Heat the oil in a large pan, add the onion and garlic and fry for about 5 minutes, until soft. Add the chilies and ginger and fry for another minute.

Stir in the ground coriander seed and turmeric, then pour in the tomato paste and water mixture. Add the marrow chunks, turning to coat in the sauce, then season to taste with salt and bring to a boil. Reduce the heat, cover, and let simmer gently for about 10 minutes, stirring occasionally.

Uncover the pan and cook for another 5 minutes, until the marrow is tender. Check the seasoning, stir in the lemon juice, and serve, with the chopped fresh cilantro sprinkled over the top.

corn

Like peas, corn is best eaten as soon as possible after picking, as the sugars start to turn rapidly to starch when the cobs have been harvested. A type of maize, corn is a summer treat that stretches into early autumn. Whole ears can be boiled or barbecued until tender, then served whole, drenched in butter and seasoned with salt and freshly ground black pepper—a truly wonderful experience, as the sweet juicy kernels explode in your mouth and mingle with the spicy pepper and lush creamy butter.

The kernels can also be stripped off the cob and used in numerous dishes. They are a great addition to the delicious cornbreads and corn puddings of the South, and are no less out of place in corn fritters, creamy chowders, spicy curries, or light refreshing salads.

Baby corncobs—just a couple of inches long—are immature cobs, picked before they are fully grown. They can be eaten whole, either raw or lightly cooked, in salads or served with dips. They are also fabulous tossed into stir-fries.

Buy the freshest corn possible, preferably still in its green husks, which must be stripped off, along with the silky threads underneath, before cooking. Then simply cook in a pot of boiling water for 5-10 minutes, until the kernels are tender. If just the kernels are needed, hold the cob upright on a board and, with a sharp knife, strip them away from the cob with a downward motion.

roast corn with chili butter

Barbecued corncobs are one of the great pleasures of summer and are especially good served with zesty chili and lime butter.

First prepare the butter, by beating together ¼ cup (½ stick) of softened butter with 1 finely chopped, seeded red chili, and the grated rind of 1½ limes. Shape into a log, wrap in plastic wrap, and let chill in the fridge for at least 30 minutes to firm up.

Meanwhile, soak the unhusked corn in cold water for 15 minutes. Drain well, then roast on a rack over the glowing coals of a barbecue for 15-20 minutes, turning from time to time, until they are cooked on all sides and the kernels are tender. To serve, pull away the husks and silky threads and enjoy the corn dotted with the chili butter.

NOTES

Corn chowder

SERVES 4

2 tbsp. olive oil
1 onion, chopped
2 cloves garlic, chopped
2 red chilies, seeded and chopped
kernels from 4 ears of corn (about 3½ cups)
11 oz. potatoes, cut up
3½ cups vegetable or chicken stock
1¾ cups milk
¼ cup heavy cream
handful of fresh flat-leaf parsley, chopped
salt and freshly ground black pepper

Heat the oil in a pan, then add the onion and garlic and fry gently for about 5 minutes. Stir in the chilies and cook for 1-2 minutes, then add the corn kernels, potatoes, and stock. Bring to a boil, reduce the heat, and let simmer for 10-15 minutes, until the corn and potatoes are tender.

Transfer about a quarter of the soup to a food processor or blender and blend until smooth. Pour back into the pot and stir to combine well.

Add the milk and heat gently until almost at a simmer. Remove from the heat, stir in the cream and chopped parsley, season to taste with salt and pepper, and serve.

Corn salad with chili, bell peppers, herbs, and smoked trout

SERVES 4

1 green chili, seeded and finely chopped
grated rind and juice of 1 lime
2 tbsp. sunflower oil
salt
4 ears of corn
1 red bell pepper, seeded and diced
3 smoked trout fillets, about 6 oz. each
large handful of fresh cilantro, roughly chopped

First make the dressing. Whisk together the chili, lime rind and juice, oil, and a pinch of salt in a small bowl. Set aside.

Bring a pot of water to a boil. Strip the husks and silky threads from the corncobs and add them to the pot. Return to a boil, then lower the heat and let simmer for 5-10 minutes until the kernels are tender. Drain, refresh under cold water, and pat dry.

Hold each cob upright on a board and, using a sharp knife, slice downwards to remove the kernels. Discard the shaved cobs.

Put the kernels in a bowl along with the red bell pepper and flake the trout fillets on top. Sprinkle the chopped cilantro over it, then pour in the dressing and toss lightly to combine. Serve.

shallots

Shallots are a member of the onion family. In season well into autumn, they are much smaller than most varieties of onion and also have a more potent flavor. The four most common varieties are the long, torpedo-shaped banana shallots, the pungent pink shallots with their reddish skin and pinky flesh, the mild brown shallots that tend to be divided into separate bulbs inside the skin, and the pungent, red Asian shallots that are often pounded into curry pastes along with other spices.

Like onions, shallots are frequently used to add an extra tang to sauces, stews, and dressings, but they can also be enjoyed as an ingredient in their own right. Try them pickled, caramelized, roasted, or used as a savory tart filling. Their intense flavor makes them useful for adding to sauces where you want extra flavor, without the bulk that would come from using onions.

Roast shallot, tomato, and thyme salad (opposite)

SERVES 4
2 tbsp. olive oil
1 tbsp. balsamic vinegar
1 tsp. soft brown sugar
12 oz. shallots (about 11–12), peeled
salt and freshly ground black pepper
12 oz. cherry tomatoes, cut in half (about 2–2½ cups)
2 large handfuls of arugula and watercress leaves
¼ cup shaved Parmesan cheese

FOR THE DRESSING
leaves from a few sprigs of fresh thyme
½ clove garlic, crushed
½ tbsp. red wine vinegar
4 tsp. olive oil

Heat the oven to 400°F. In a small bowl, whisk together the olive oil, balsamic vinegar, and sugar. Put the shallots in a baking dish, then drizzle the oil and vinegar mixture over them and toss to coat. Season with salt and pepper and roast in the oven for about 30 minutes, shaking the dish once or twice during the cooking time, until tender and browned.

Meanwhile, prepare the dressing. Gently bruise the thyme leaves in a mortar, then add the garlic, red wine vinegar, and olive oil, and whisk together. Season with salt and pepper and set aside.

Put the tomatoes and roasted shallots in a bowl. Drizzle with the dressing and toss to combine. Divide the arugula and watercress leaves among four serving plates, spoon the tomatoes and shallots on top, and scatter with the Parmesan shavings. Serve immediately.

NOTES

beets

Dark-purple beets with their rich, magenta juice and sweet flavor are available for most of the year—either in season in summer and fall, or from the cold-store throughout the winter. Beets range from tiny globes to roots the size of a fist, with a fat, rounded shape narrowing to a delicate point at the whispy root-end. Buy it with the delicate, pink-tinged green leaves still attached, if you can, as these can be used like spinach or added to salads.

Beets are wonderfully versatile. They make a good vegetable in their own right and are excellent pureed to create a warming, hearty soup, or even an elegant, chilled one. They can also be chopped and tossed into stews and roasted or baked with other roots until sweet and juicy. Their mild, sweet flavor makes a good foil for any sharp, salty ingredients in a dish and the juice will leach out, giving an attractive reddish-purple hue. For a delicious, eye-catching salad, try pairing beets with juicy orange segments, slices of red onion, and a sprinkling of zesty mint, or go for an East European touch by mixing it with pickled herrings, sour cream, and fresh dill.

When buying, look for firm, undamaged specimens, and try to buy roots of an even size for ease of cooking. Twist off the leaves and wash gently under the faucet. Then boil or bake in a moderate oven until tender. The skin will slip off easily after cooking and should be discarded.

baked beets

One of the simplest ways to cook beets is to bake them in a lightly spiced olive oil dressing until sweet and tender. Trim and peel 6 medium-sized beets, then cut into quarters—or wedges, if large—and put in a baking dish. Whisk together 1 tablespoon of balsamic vinegar, 2 tablespoons of olive oil, 1 teaspoon of ground cumin, and 1 finely chopped clove of garlic, then season with salt and freshly ground black pepper. Pour this mixture over the beets, then toss to coat. Bake in a heated oven at 400°F for about 40 minutes, turning once or twice during cooking, until tender. Serve hot, warm, or cold, sprinkled with a handful of chopped fresh mint or parsley.

NOTES

Beet salad with broiled halloumi

SERVES 4

7 oz. halloumi cheese, sliced into
¼-inch-thick slices
1 red chili, seeded and
finely chopped
1 clove garlic, crushed
juice of 1 lemon
3 tbsp. olive oil
1 tbsp. red wine vinegar
pinch of sugar
grated rind of ½ lemon
1½ tsp. chopped fresh mint leaves
salt and freshly ground black pepper
4 oz. corn salad (mâche) or other
summer salad greens (about 2 large
handfuls)
11 oz. cooked beets, cut into slim
wedges

Arrange the halloumi in a dish in a single layer. Whisk together the chili, garlic, lemon juice, and 1 tablespoon of the oil in a small bowl and pour it over the halloumi. Turn to coat well, then let it marinate for at least 30 minutes.

Make a dressing by whisking together the vinegar, sugar, lemon rind, mint, and remaining olive oil in a small bowl. Season to taste with salt and pepper and set aside. Heat the broiler to hot and line the broiler pan with foil, or heat a ridged grill pan.

Divide the salad greens between four serving plates and scatter the beet wedges on top.

Place the halloumi slices on the prepared broiler pan or grill pan and cook on each side until lightly charred and just starting to bubble. Scatter the halloumi over the prepared salads. Drizzle with the dressing and serve immediately.

beet and yogurt dip

In the Middle East, beets and yogurt are frequently paired. This healthy dip takes its inspiration from that tradition. It is very quick and easy to prepare and makes a wonderful start to any summer meal.

Simply put 9 ounces of cooked beets in a food processor or blender, add ½ cup of plain yogurt, 1 teaspoon of ground coriander seed, a pinch of ground ginger, and a pinch of salt, and blend to make a smooth puree. Stir in some lemon juice to taste, then serve accompanied by breadsticks or wedges of pita bread for dipping.

NOTES

Beet and chocolate cake

Adding beets to this dark chocolate cake gives it a really rich, moist texture and a luscious, but not at all sickly, sweetness. The cinnamon and orange zest lend a subtle yet intriguing complexity to the overall flavor.

MAKES 1 x 8-INCH CAKE
one 3½-oz. bar dark chocolate
¾ cup (1½ sticks) butter, at room temperature
¾ cup soft brown sugar
3 eggs
1¼ cups all-purpose flour
2½ tsp. baking powder
½ tsp. salt
1-2 tbsp. cocoa powder
1 tsp. ground cinnamon
grated rind of 1 orange
1 large beet, about 5½ oz., peeled and grated

FOR THE ICING
one 3½-oz. bar dark chocolate, chopped
½ cup heavy cream

Heat the oven to 350°F. Lightly grease an 8-inch round cake pan and dust it with flour.

Break the chocolate into small pieces and place in the top of a double boiler over simmering water, so that the bottom of the top pan does not touch the water, and stir gently until the chocolate melts. Set aside to cool.

Beat the butter and sugar together until light and fluffy, then beat in the eggs one at a time, followed by the cooled chocolate. Sift in the flour, baking powder, salt, cocoa, and cinnamon, and fold in carefully. Fold in the orange rind and beet.

Tip the batter into the prepared pan and smooth the surface to make it even. Bake in the oven for about 50 minutes, until risen and a skewer inserted into the center comes out clean. Turn out onto a wire rack and let cool.

Meanwhile, make the icing. Put the chocolate in a heatproof bowl. Heat the cream until almost boiling, then pour it over the chocolate and let stand for about 5 minutes. Stir until the chocolate has melted and the mixture is smooth and creamy. Let cool slightly, until thick and glossy, then swirl it on top of the cake.

summer berries

Summer is always associated with an abundance of sweet fragrant berries. Strawberries and their vibrant red skins, speckled with tiny yellow seeds, arrive first, swiftly followed by soft succulent raspberries, with their velvety skin and deep pinkish-red hue, and fat juicy blueberries with their misty bloom. And there are a host of other less common berries too, including loganberries, youngberries, tayberries, and boysenberries.

Most summer berries can simply be rinsed and eaten as they are, drenched with thick cream and perhaps a sprinkling of sugar, according to taste. However, they are also wonderfully versatile and can be added to fruit salads, cakes, muffins, tarts, and pies. They are also perfect for decorating or piling on top of desserts such as meringues. And if you tire of eating them fresh, they can be preserved in jams and jellies or bottled in alcohol and sugar syrups.

Summer berry pavlova (opposite)

SERVES 6
4 egg whites
1 cup sugar
2 tsp. cornstarch
1 tsp. white wine vinegar
1¼ cups heavy cream
1 tsp. vanilla extract
2 tbsp. confectioners' sugar, plus extra for dusting
18 oz. mixed summer berries, such as blueberries, strawberries, and raspberries (about 3½–4½ cups), hulled and rinsed

Heat the oven to 275°F. Line a baking sheet with parchment paper and mark out a 10-inch-diameter circle on it.

Beat the egg whites in a clean bowl until they form stiff peaks. Gradually fold in the sugar, a tablespoon at a time, folding in the cornstarch and vinegar with the last portion of sugar.

Spoon the meringue onto the baking sheet, inside the marked circle, flatten it a little and make an indentation in the center. Bake for about 1¼ hours in the oven until firm.

Remove from the oven, let cool, then carefully peel off the paper and place the meringue on a flat plate.

Whip the cream until it stands in soft peaks, then stir in the vanilla extract. Sift in and fold in the confectioners' sugar. Spoon onto the meringue and pile the berries on top. Dust lightly with confectioners' sugar and serve.

NOTES

Raspberry millefeuille

SERVES 4

flour, for dusting
9 oz. puff pastry dough
1⅓ cups crème fraîche or
sour cream
3 tbsp. lemon curd
11 oz. raspberries (about 2 cups),
rinsed
confectioners' sugar, for dusting

Heat the oven to 400°F. Lightly grease two baking sheets. On a lightly floured surface, roll out the dough to about ¼-inch thick, then trim to a 12 x 6-inch rectangle. Slice the dough into six rectangles of 4 x 3 inches and arrange these on the baking sheets. Bake in the oven for 10 minutes until puffed up and golden. Transfer to a wire rack to cool.

Meanwhile, fold the crème fraîche and lemon curd together, then leave in the fridge to chill until ready to assemble the pastries.

With a serrated knife, cut each pastry rectangle in half horizontally and arrange four halves on a serving platter. Spread each with a couple of spoonfuls of the lemon cream, then top with some raspberries and a second pastry half. Repeat with more lemon cream and berries, then a third pastry half. Dust with confectioners' sugar and serve.

Blueberry and almond muffins

MAKES 12

3 cups all-purpose flour
4 tsp. baking powder
1½ tsp. salt
¾ cup sugar
2 eggs, beaten
½ cup milk
¼ cup vegetable oil
¼ tsp. almond extract (optional)
1 cup. blueberries
2 tbsp. slivered almonds

Heat the oven to 400°F. Line a 12-cup muffin pan with paper muffin cups.

Sift the flour and sugar together into a large mixing bowl. Make a well in the center and set aside.

Put the eggs, milk, oil, and almond extract, if using, in a large measuring cup and beat together to combine. Pour into the well in the flour mixture and stir vigorously to combine. It does not matter if the mixture is a little lumpy.

Drop a tablespoon of the mixture into the bottom of each paper cup, then sprinkle in a few blueberries. Top with the remaining batter, then more blueberries, pressing them gently into the batter. Sprinkle a few almond slivers over each muffin.

Bake in the oven for about 20 minutes until risen and golden. Transfer to a wire rack to cool slightly before serving.

NOTES

Baby summer puddings

This classic English dessert of bread and berries is an excellent way to use up bread in the summer without having to turn on the oven—a summer bread pudding.

SERVES 4

6 thin slices day-old white bread, crusts removed

18 oz. mixed summer berries, such as raspberries, strawberries, blueberries, black currants, and red currants

about 4 tsp. sugar

3 tbsp. water

juice of ¼ lemon

thick cream or whipped cream, for serving

Trim the bread slices and use to line the bottoms and sides of four small timbale molds or ramekins (about ¾ cup each). Cut out four circles from the remaining bread to fit inside the top of the molds and set aside.

Prepare the fruit by removing any stems, leaves, and hulls, and cutting any large berries into halves or quarters. Put in a pan and sprinkle in the sugar and water. Cover tightly and heat very gently, shaking occasionally, for 5 minutes, until the berries start to release their juices. Increase the heat slightly and cook for another 4 minutes, shaking the pan frequently, until the juices are released and syrupy.

Remove from the heat, check the flavoring, and add the lemon juice and more sugar if necessary. Let cool slightly, then spoon the fruit along with a little juice into the bread-lined molds. Reserve any remaining juice.

Place one of the reserved circles of bread on top of each pudding, then put a small saucer on top of that and weigh it down with something heavy. Chill in the fridge for at least 4 hours.

To serve, run a knife between each pudding and its mold and carefully turn out onto serving plates. Spoon any reserved juice over the top and serve with thick cream or whipped cream.

marinated strawberries

Marinating strawberries with a drizzle of sweet, caramely balsamic vinegar really helps to bring out their sweetness and produces a wonderfully rich flavor.

To prepare, hull and cut in half about 5 cups of ripe strawberries, then sprinkle in 1 teaspoon of sugar and 1½ teaspoons of balsamic vinegar. Toss to combine, then cover and chill for about 1 hour before serving. Try with ice cream or a slice of cheesecake or a creamy panna cotta, or just as they are.

currants

Tiny, jewel-like currants—glossy black, ruby red, and creamy white—are among the delights of late summer. They look stunning piled on top of fresh fruit tarts, cakes, pavlovas, and other desserts and add a delicious, sharp tang when mixed with sweeter, softer berries, such as strawberries. Although each type has a distinct individual flavor, all currants are tart. White currants, being the least acidic, are pleasant eaten raw, but in general currants are best served cooked—in sauces, in desserts (such as summer pudding, see page 115), and in jams and jellies. Currant sauces and jellies are frequently served with game, the tartness of the fruit making a good foil for the richness of the meat.

Buy only plump, shiny currants. To prepare, simply strip the berries from their stalks. The easiest way to do this is to hold the stalk by the stem, then strip it through the tines of a fork, so that the currants are gently pulled off.

Black currant sherbet

SERVES 4-6
1 lb. black currants, rinsed and trimmed (about 4½ cups), plus extra for decorating
300ml/10½fl oz./1¼ cups water
¾ cup sugar
3 tbsp. crème de cassis liqueur
1 egg white

Put the black currants in a pan with half the water. Cover and simmer for about 5 minutes, until the fruit is tender. Set aside to cool slightly.

Put the cooled currants in a food processor or blender and blend to make a smooth puree, then press through a fine mesh strainer to remove any debris. Chill in the fridge for at least 1 hour.

Meanwhile, put the remaining water and the sugar in a pan and heat, stirring, until the sugar has dissolved. Remove from the heat and let cool, then chill. When the puree and syrup are thoroughly chilled, stir together with the crème de cassis.

Pour the mixture into an ice cream maker and churn until thick, then add the egg white and continue churning until the mixture is thick enough to scoop.

To make by hand, freeze the mixture for 4 hours, then blend in a food processor until smooth. Lightly whisk the egg white until frothy, fold into the mixture, then freeze until firm.

Serve decorated with fresh black currants.

NOTES

gooseberries

Although it is the tart green fruits that most people think of when gooseberries are mentioned, there are golden and red varieties, too—all of them perfect for summer desserts. The early-season green gooseberries are tart and sharp and should be cooked until tender with plenty of sugar. However, the ripe golden and red gooseberries can be sweet and mild and may be eaten raw. Cooked gooseberries are commonly paired with fragrant elderflowers—their white clustered heads can be seen growing in hedgerows alongside country fields and lanes.

Gooseberries are frequently used in pies, tarts, and creamy fools, and preserved in jams and jellies. They can also be made into a wonderfully tart sauce, which is a popular accompaniment to broiled mackerel, contrasting well with the oiliness of the fish.

To prepare gooseberries, simply top and tail them with a pair of kitchen scissors, then use them according to the recipe. If you are making a puree by straining the cooked berries, you can skip the topping and tailing since the debris will be removed with straining.

Gooseberry fool

The amount of sugar needed for this traditional English pudding will depend on the type of gooseberry you use—and personal taste, of course—so just keep adding sugar once the berries are cooked to attain the desired sweet-sour balance.

SERVES 4
1 lb. gooseberries (about 3 cups), topped and tailed
2 tbsp. water
sugar, to taste
½ cup heavy cream
⅔ cup Greek yogurt or thick whole-milk yogurt

Put the gooseberries and water in a pan, cover, and heat over a low heat until the juices start to run. Uncover, bring to a boil, then reduce the heat and simmer for about 10 minutes, stirring occasionally, until tender.

Remove from the heat, mash, and stir in sugar to taste, then let cool completely.

Whip the cream in a large bowl, then fold the Greek yogurt into it, followed by the cooled gooseberries. Serve cold or chilled.

NOTES

Gooseberry and elderflower preserve

Tart gooseberries and fragrant elderflowers are a classic pairing. Serve this delicious preserve for an elegant traditional afternoon tea, spread generously on thick slices of bread and butter.

MAKES ABOUT 4½ LB.
2¼ lb. gooseberries, topped and tailed
1 cup water
5 cups granulated sugar
juice of 1 lemon
flowers from 4 elderflower heads

Put the gooseberries in a large pot and pour in the water. Bring to a boil, reduce the heat, cover, and let simmer for about 20 minutes, until the fruit is tender, then crush it using the back of a spoon.

Add the sugar, lemon juice, and elderflowers, and stir over a low heat until the sugar has dissolved. Boil for about 10 minutes until the temperature reaches 220°F on a candy thermometer, then skim off any scum from the surface. Let cool for 5-10 minutes, then ladle into sterilized jars and seal.

elderflowers

The white clustered flowers of the elderberry tree have an intense, perfumed flavor. They can be used in many recipes to add a delicious scented touch. A few flowerheads may be added to the pan when making jam, for instance, and stirred in until enough flavor has been imparted. Then fish out the flowers and continue making the jam in the usual way. They are also commonly used to prepare a syrup, that is diluted with sparking spring water to make a refreshing drink, or used to flavor desserts. Use only flowers with creamy open petals that are not yet beginning to drop.

To prepare elderflower syrup, put 2 pounds of sugar (2⅔ cups) in a large bowl and pour in 10 cups of boiling water. Stir to dissolve, then let cool. Stir in 1 package of citric acid, then rinse 30 elderflower heads and add to the sugar syrup with 2 thinly sliced lemons. Let stand for 24 hours, stirring occasionally. Strain the liquid through a jelly bag or double thickness cheesecloth and bottle it. This syrup freezes well, too.

cherries

The arrival of cherry blossom always seems to mark the beginning of spring and, in the same way, the arrival of shiny plump cherries, piled high on the produce shelves, tells us that summer is truly here. From creamy yellow through bright red to dark purple-black, these wonderful fruits, hanging in twos and threes from long narrow stalks, are the ultimate seasonal treat. They may be sweet or sour according to variety—although only the sweet ones are usually on sale—and the flesh can vary from firm and crisp to soft and juicy.

Sweet cherries are usually eaten raw, while the intensely flavored sour ones are reserved for cooking—mainly in preserves—or for making liqueurs. Cherries have a natural affinity with chocolate and the two ingredients feature together in numerous desserts, most famously in the creamy chocolate cake Black Forest torte. Fresh cherries may be pitted and folded into cake batter before baking. The pitted fruits are also good in pies, tarts, strudels, and other baked desserts, or frozen into sherbets and ice creams. They make a sharp fruity sauce to serve with game and, in Eastern Europe, are widely used to make sweet-and-sour soups and as a stuffing for dumplings.

Buy only plump glossy fruits with unblemished skins and flexible green stalks. Any with browning or brittle stalks indicate that the cherries were picked quite some time ago. Flavor can vary enormously, so, if you can, taste before you buy. Cherries take little preparation and should simply be washed and plucked from their stalk. Some recipes call for the pits to be removed. The easiest way to do this is with a cherry pitter, in which the cherry sits in a tiny cup and a bar is pressed through the center of the fruit, pushing out the pit. If you do not have a cherry pitter, cut around the pit (as you would for larger pitted fruits, such as peaches and apricots), then gently pull away the flesh and pry out the pit.

NOTES

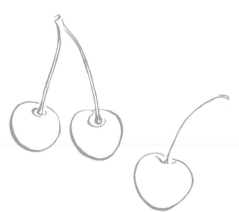

Cherry chocolate brownies

Dark chocolate and juicy cherries are natural partners and these luscious brownies—sweet, sticky, and studded with fresh cherries—are truly indulgent. Serve them unadorned, or with thick cream or ice cream. When fresh cherries are out of season, make the brownies with drained preserved cherries (see page 123), substituting the kirsch with the preserving liqueur.

MAKES 16

two 3½-oz. bars dark chocolate
¾ cup plus 2 tbsp. (1¾ sticks) butter
3 eggs
1 cup sugar
2 tbsp. kirsch liqueur
½ cup all-purpose flour
7 oz. fresh cherries, pitted (about 1¼ cups)

Heat the oven to 350°F. Grease a 9-inch square baking pan and dust with flour.

Put the chocolate and butter in the top of a double boiler over simmering water, so that the bottom of the top pan does not touch the water, and warm, stirring, until the chocolate has nearly melted. Remove from the heat and continue stirring until the chocolate has completely melted. Set aside to cool for about 5-10 minutes.

Beat the eggs into the chocolate mixture, one at a time, then stir in the sugar and kirsch. Sift in the flour, then fold it in. Fold in the cherries. Turn the batter into the prepared pan and spread out evenly. Bake in the oven for about 30 minutes, until pale and slightly crackled on top and just firm to the touch.

Let the brownies cool in the pan, then cut into squares.

chocolate-dipped cherries

Fresh cherries dipped in either dark or white chocolate make wonderful *petits fours* to serve with coffee after a special dinner. They are also quick and easy to prepare. Simply break some chocolate into small pieces and place in the top of a double boiler over simmering water, making sure the bottom of the top pan is not touching the water, and stir gently until the chocolate has melted. Remove the top pan from the heat. Holding each cherry by its stem, dip the bottom half into the melted chocolate, then place on a baking sheet lined with waxed paper. Leave in a cool place to set, then chill in the fridge until ready to serve.

Clafoutis (opposite)

This melt-in-the-mouth, custardy French batter pudding is a wonderful way to make the most of the glut of fresh cherries available during their brief season. Traditionally it is made with a particular variety of black cherry known as a *guine*, but any type of black cherry can be used here to make a heavenly dessert. Some prefer to pit the cherries before adding them to the dish for ease of eating, but leaving them in gives a better flavor.

SERVES 4-6
butter, for greasing
11 oz. black cherries
(about 1½-2 cups)
⅓ cup all-purpose flour
¼ cup sugar
6 large eggs, beaten
1 cup milk
¾ cup light cream
2 tbsp. kirsch liqueur
confectioners' sugar, for dusting

Heat the oven to 375°F. Butter a round baking dish, about 8 inches in diameter, and scatter the cherries in the bottom.

Combine the flour and sugar in a bowl, then gradually beat in the eggs until smooth. Whisk in the milk and cream, then stir in the kirsch. Pour this batter over the cherries and bake in the oven for about 50 minutes, until golden and puffed up. It should still have a wobble, but a knife inserted in the center should come out clean. Serve hot or warm, dusted with confectioners' sugar.

preserving cherries

Cherries are in season for only a few short months, so it is well worth preserving them in jams, jellies, and other sweet and savory preserves when they are available in abundance. They may be bottled in sugar and alcohol to make a sweet cherry liqueur, the alcohol-spiked cherries being a glorious addition to chocolate cakes, ice cream, and other creamy desserts. They even make lovely sour pickles, when preserved with vinegar and spices, to serve with red meats and game.

To preserve cherries in brandy, wash and pit about 1 pound of cherries (about 2½-3 cups) and pack into a wide-necked bottle or jar, sprinkling in 6 tablespoons of granulated sugar as you go. Pour in enough brandy to cover, and seal tightly. Store in a cool, dark place for at least 1 month, shaking the bottle occasionally, before serving.

apricots

Native to China, peachy orange apricots with their velvety skin thrive in warmer climates. Arriving for a brief season in early summer, they are generally best cooked—either poached, baked, or roasted—so that the flesh becomes meltingly tender and juicy with a sweet yet refreshingly sharp flavor.

Try them in compotes and fruit salads, tarts and pies, and cakes and crumbles, or make them into ice creams and mousses. They are delicious preserved in jellies and jams—stirring just a spoonful or two of homemade apricot jam through plain yogurt makes a quick and simple dessert that can be enjoyed at any time of the year.

Large quantities of apricots are also preserved by drying, which often helps to intensify their flavor. Dried apricots are a popular additon to many savory dishes, such as meat stews and pilafs, and are mixed into stuffings for meat and poultry, as in many Middle Eastern recipes.

Select firm ripe fruits with an almost glowing color and avoid any that are bruised, blemished, or have a greenish tinge. To remove the pit, cut around the crease of the fruit using a sharp knife, then twist the two halves apart and pry out the pit.

roast apricots

One of the simplest and most delicious ways to enjoy apricots is to roast them. They can then be served hot from the oven with a big spoonful of crème fraîche or another cream, or served cold, stirred into plain yogurt or with ice cream. They are also delicious on slices of toasted *panettone* or raisin bread for breakfast.

To prepare, allow 3 apricots per person. Cut them in half and pit them, then arrange, cut-side up, in a baking dish. Sprinkle a few teaspoons of sugar over each half and then bake in a heated oven at 400°F for about 30 minutes until tender and juicy.

NOTES

Apricot and almond tart

Juicy tart apricots and sweet crunchy almonds are a classic combination—as you will soon realize for good reason, when you tuck into this sublime tart.

SERVES 6-8

½ cup (1 stick) butter, at room temperature
½ cup sugar
2 eggs
1¼ cups ground almonds
grated rind of ½ lemon
11 oz. fresh apricots, cut in half and pitted (about 1½-2 cups)
confectioners' sugar, for dusting

FOR THE PASTRY DOUGH

a scant cup all-purpose flour, plus extra for dusting
½ tbsp. sugar
¼ cup (½ stick) butter, chilled and diced
about 1 tbsp. cold water

First make the pastry dough. Put the flour and sugar in a food processor and pulse to combine. Add the butter and pulse until the mixture resembles fine bread crumbs. With the motor running, gradually add just enough water until the mixture comes together. Press into a ball, wrap in plastic wrap and leave in the fridge to chill for at least 30 minutes.

Heat the oven to 375°F. On a lightly floured surface, roll out the dough and line an 8-inch tart pan. Cover the pie shell with foil and baking beans and bake in the oven for 10 minutes. Remove the foil and beans and bake for a 5-10 minutes more until the bottom is dry. Remove from the oven and lower the temperature to 350°F.

Meanwhile, beat the butter and sugar together in a large bowl, then beat in the eggs, one at a time. Fold in the ground almonds and lemon rind, then spoon the mixture into the prepared pie shell. Arrange the apricots in the tart, gently pressing them into the almond mixture. Bake for about 35 minutes, until firm and golden brown. Serve warm or cold, lightly dusted with confectioners' sugar.

apricot and marzipan phyllo dough bundles

To make a simple and delicious dessert for four people, cut 8 apricots in half and remove the pits. Place a piece of marzipan into the gap left by the pit in each fruit, then press the apricot halves back together around it. Take 2 sheets of phyllo pastry dough, brush with melted butter, then place one on top of the other and trim into an 8-inch square. Put an apricot in the center, pull up the pastry dough around the fruit, and twist to form a small bundle. Repeat with more pastry dough sheets and the rest of the apricots. Brush the bundles with more butter, then arrange on a baking sheet and bake in a heated oven at 350°F for about 25 minutes until crisp and golden. Serve warm, lightly dusted with confectioners' sugar.

peaches and nectarines

Succulent peaches and nectarines need plenty of sunshine to develop their luscious sweetness and are at their best when left to ripen fully on the tree. The two fruits are similar in taste and texture and can generally be substituted for each other. The main difference is in their skin. Peaches are covered in a soft downy bloom while the skin of nectarines is smooth and glossy like that of plums. Both fruits may have either white or yellow flesh, the white-fleshed varieties generally being considered to have the better flavor.

Delicious eaten straight from the tree, they can also be sliced or chopped and added to salads and desserts. They are good cooked, too—poached, broiled, or roasted and baked into pies, crumbles, and cobblers, or preserved by simply canning in syrup or alcohol or making into jam.

Choose unblemished fruits that give slightly when squeezed gently in the palm of the hand. If peeled peaches or nectarines are called for, place the fruits in a heatproof bowl and cover with boiling water. Let stand for about 15 seconds. Drain, then slip off and discard the skins.

Peaches in white wine and vanilla syrup

SERVES 4
4 peaches, about 1½ lb. in total
1½ cups white wine
1 cup granulated sugar
1 vanilla bean
3 tbsp. brandy
thick cream or ice cream,
for serving

Put the peaches in a large heatproof bowl and cover with boiling water. Leave for about 15 seconds, then drain and peel away the skins. Cut in half, and remove and discard the pits.

Put the wine and sugar in a pan. Split the vanilla bean lengthwise, then add to the pan. Heat, stirring, until the sugar has dissolved. Bring to a boil and let bubble for 5 minutes, then add the prepared peaches, cover, and simmer for 5-10 minutes until the fruit is just tender.

Remove the peaches from the pan and place in a serving bowl, then remove and discard the vanilla bean. Boil the syrup for 5-10 minutes until reduced and slightly thickened. Remove from the heat, stir in the brandy, and pour it over the peaches. Let cool. Serve at room temperature or chilled with cream or ice cream.

NOTES

melons

Available from summer to early fall, fragrant melons, with their refreshing honeyed flesh, grow on trailing vines and come in many guises: cantaloupes, with their ridged rind and apricot-tinted flesh; crenshaws, with their sweet pale-orange interior; casabas, with their pale green flesh and crumpled skin; the roundish smooth-skinned honeydews, with their pale-green skin and flesh; and watermelons, with their thirst-quenching, bright-red flesh—to name but a few. Melons vary enormously in size, too. Some are just big enough for one or two people, while others, such as watermelons, can be huge and are often sold cut into wedges rather than whole. Usually eaten raw, they can be perfect on their own, or simply sprinkled with a little ground ginger, or spiked with a few drops of alcohol. The flesh is also good sliced or chopped into salads, or juiced with other fruits and vegetables. It is delicious pureed and blended into chilled summer soups, turned into sherbets, or used to make melon jam. The rind, which is usually discarded, can even be preserved in vinegar and spices and served as a pickle.

Choose fruits that feel heavy for their size. When ripe, most melons have a strong fragrant aroma, so try to hold and smell them before buying. Avoid those with little or no scent or a musky smell which indicates that the fruit may be over-ripe. To prepare, cut small melons in half, and cut larger ones into wedges. Then scoop out and discard the seeds, but for watermelons, where the seeds are embedded in the flesh, these can be easily removed with a pointed knife.

spiked watermelon

Alcohol-spiked melon is great for a summer party. Use an apple corer or long vegetable peeler to make six bore-holes in the top of a melon, reserving the cored-out pieces. Press a wooden skewer into each bore-hole several times at different angles to make fine channels into the flesh. Pour vodka into each bore-hole and let the melon absorb the alcohol. Top up from time to time, using about 2 cups vodka in total. Replace the removed pieces and leave in a cool place overnight. Serve sliced into wedges.

NOTES

Cantaloupe and feta salad

This light refreshing salad of sweet juicy melon, studded with cubes of salty cheese, makes a delicious summer appetizer. You can use any kind of melon but fragrant cantaloupe, with its apricot-colored flesh, looks particularly attractive.

SERVES 4

juice and grated rind of ½ lemon
pinch of sugar
3 tbsp. olive oil
freshly ground black pepper
2 tsp. finely chopped fresh mint leaves
2 ripe cantaloupes
4 oz. feta cheese, cut into bite-size cubes (about 1 cup)
2 tbsp. pine nuts, toasted

Make a dressing by whisking together the lemon juice and rind, sugar, and olive oil in a small bowl. Season to taste with pepper, stir in the chopped mint, and set aside.

Cut the cantaloupes in half and scoop out the seeds. Then cut into wedges and slice off and discard the skin. Chop the wedges of melon flesh into bite-size chunks.

Divide the melon among four serving plates and scatter the feta cheese and pine nuts over them. Drizzle with the dressing and serve.

Melon sherbet

Use ripe scented melon with a good flavor for this sherbet. Any kind will do—casabas, cantaloupes, and watermelons all work equally well.

SERVES 4

2 tbsp. sugar
¼ cup water
1 melon, about 1½ lb.
juice of 1 lime
few sprigs of fresh mint, for decorating

Put the sugar and water in a pan and heat gently, stirring, until the sugar dissolves, then bring to a boil. Remove from the heat and set aside to cool.

Cut the melon into wedges, scoop out the seeds, then cut the melon flesh from the skin. Chop the flesh into rough chunks, then place in a food processor or blender and blend to make a smooth puree. Stir in the cooled sugar syrup and lime juice.

Churn the mixture in an ice cream maker until it is thick and smooth, then freeze until firm and scoopable. Serve, decorated with sprigs of fresh mint.

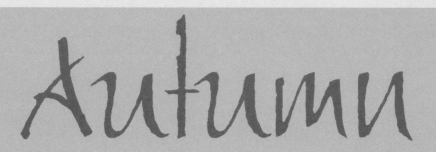

Autumn

After long days of summer sunshine, the coolness of autumn ushers in a bumper harvest. Golden-orange squashes, sweet potatoes, earthy wild mushrooms, anise-seedy fennel, and crisp celery all come into season. They are perfect for cooking up into more substantial dishes as the temperatures begins to drop. Wild game is also one of the many pleasures that arrive with the fall. Venison, rabbit, duck, quail, pheasant, and pigeon are just a few of the treats available—each with its own robust and distinctive flavor and perfect for roasting, braising, or stewing with the many and varied seasonal vegetables and fruits. The appearance of plump honeyed figs, purple-bloomed plums, and scented grapes may mark the end of summer's glut of berries, but they are a wonderful way to welcome in the new season. Jewel-like pomegranates are a joy to the eye, as well as adding a refreshing tang to both sweet and savory dishes. There are heaps of apples and pears, and the hedgerows are bulging with wild fruits, just waiting to be picked and turned into jams and jellies.

onions

Onions are available from cold-storage at any time of the year, but appear in the stores freshly harvested only from late summer until late autumn. They are one of those true kitchen essentials. Virtually every savory recipe—from soups, sauces, and stews to curries and tagines—uses onions as a flavoring. But they are more than just a necessary addition to a dish; they can also be the central feature, as the many superb recipes for onion soups, onion tarts, roasted and stuffed onions, onion pakoras, and crispy fried onion rings all demonstrate. As a general rule, most onions have a crisp, juicy texture and powerful, pungent flavor when raw, but become soft, mild, and sweet when cooked.

There are many different varieties of onion, all with their own distinctive characteristics. Brown onions with their thickish skins are the real kitchen standby. Their strong flavor mellows to an almost caramel-like sweetness when they are gently fried. Large, round Spanish—or yellow—onions have a much milder flavor that becomes honeyed with long slow cooking. Red onions are milder still, making them ideal for using raw or in dishes that require only a short cooking time. White onions, with their papery skin and white flesh, usually have a fairly pungent flavor. Smaller onions, such as the tiny white pearl variety and the distinctive flat cipolla—or *borettane*—onions are usually used whole for pickling or in stews.

When buying, select only firm onions, avoiding any that are damaged or starting to soften. They keep well, so it is worth buying a string of them if you can. Hang this somewhere suitably cool and dark, and it should last for several months.

Onions are nearly always peeled before using. They can be cooked whole, sliced, or chopped. To peel large onions, simply slice off the top and bottom, then make a shallow slit in the skin and peel it away. To peel the smaller pearl onions, slice off the top and bottom as for larger onions, then soak in boiling water for about 3 minutes to loosen the skins, which should then slip off easily.

NOTES

Pissaladière

This classic French tart, topped with meltingly sweet onions and salty anchovies and olives, is often made with a pie crust, but it is equally good on a crisp yeasted dough.

SERVES 6

2 tbsp. olive oil
3 Spanish onions, thinly sliced
2 cloves garlic, sliced
4-6 fresh sage leaves, chopped
salt and freshly ground black pepper
2-oz. can anchovies, drained and cut in half lengthwise
large handful of juicy black olives
handful of golden raisins

FOR THE YEAST DOUGH

2⅓ cups white bread flour, plus extra for dusting
½ tsp. salt
1½ tsp. rapid-rise dried yeast
¾ cup warm water
2 tbsp. olive oil

First make the yeast dough. Combine the flour, salt, and yeast in a bowl and make a well in the center. Pour the water and oil into the well and gradually mix in the flour mixture to make a soft, but not sticky, dough. Tip out onto a lightly floured surface and knead for about 10 minutes, until smooth and elastic. Place in a clean bowl, cover with plastic wrap and let rise for about 45 minutes, until doubled in size.

Meanwhile, heat the oil in a pan, add the onions and garlic, and cook gently over a very low heat for about 25 minutes, stirring frequently, until very tender and collapsed. Sprinkle in the sage, season with salt and pepper, and remove from the heat.

Heat the oven to 425°F and grease a baking sheet. Roll out the dough to form a rectangle about 12 x 10 inches. Place on the baking sheet, spread with the onion mixture, then arrange the anchovies and olives on top. Bake in the oven for about 10 minutes, then scatter the raisins over it and return to the oven for another 10 minutes, until the dough is golden and crispy. Serve warm, cut into slices.

french onion soup

This satisfying soup is a perfect way to welcome in the first onions of the fall. Topped with cheesy croûtes, it is almost a meal in itself. The secret to the rich color and flavor lies in caramelizing the onions. To prepare, cook about 6 thinly sliced onions in 2 tablespoons of olive oil over a low heat, stirring frequently, for about 20 minutes, until the onions are very soft. Stir in a sprinkling of fresh thyme, a good pinch of soft brown sugar, and 2 tablespoons of balsamic vinegar, then continue cooking and stirring for another 20 minutes, until the mixture is dark and sticky—don't let it burn. Stir in 1 tablespoon of flour, then gradually add 4 cups of beef or vegetable stock and 1 cup of white wine. Simmer, covered, for 15 minutes, then check and adjust the seasoning.

Make the croûtes by heating 4 ounces of Gruyère (or Swiss) cheese (about 1 cup), a splash of white wine, and a little Dijon mustard together in a pan until the cheese melts. Remove from the heat and beat in an egg yolk. Spoon this mixture over 4 thick slices of toasted baguette that have been rubbed with garlic, and broil these until golden and bubbling. Serve the soup piping hot, with a cheesy croûte floating on top of each bowl.

Creamy red onion and Parmesan tart (opposite)

Onions make the perfect filling for savory tarts and pies—and red ones are wonderful, as here, roasted until sweet and caramelized and paired with a garlicky, cheesy egg custard.

SERVES 6
¼ cup milk
⅓ cup light cream
2 cloves garlic, cut in half
2 red onions
2 tbsp. olive oil
1 tbsp. balsamic vinegar
salt and freshly ground black pepper
1 egg yolk
1 tbsp. all-purpose flour, plus extra for dusting
½ cup grated Parmesan cheese
13 oz. puff pastry dough
handful of black olives
2 tsp. capers, rinsed and patted dry
leaves from 2-3 sprigs of fresh thyme

Heat the oven to 400°F. Grease a baking sheet. Put the milk, cream, and garlic in a pan and bring to a boil, then remove from the heat and let stand for 15 minutes.

Meanwhile, peel the red onions and, keeping the root intact, cut each one into 6-8 wedges and arrange in a roasting tin. Whisk together the oil and vinegar, drizzle it over the onions and turn them to coat. Season with salt and pepper and roast in the oven for 15 minutes. Remove from the oven, set aside, and lower the temperature to 375°F.

Whisk together the egg yolk and flour in a heatproof bowl to make a smooth paste. Bring the milk and cream back to simmering point, then remove the garlic and discard. Gradually pour the hot milk and cream into the egg and flour mixture, whisking continuously, until well combined and really smooth. Return to the pan and heat gently for about 3 minutes, stirring constantly, until thick and creamy. Remove from the heat, stir in the Parmesan cheese, and season to taste with salt and pepper.

Roll out the dough on a lightly floured surface, cut out a 10-inch circle, and place on the baking sheet. Spread the cheesy custard over the dough, leaving a ¾-inch border all the way around, then arrange the roasted onions on top. Scatter the olives and capers on top and bake in the oven for about 25 minutes, until the crust is crisp and golden. Serve, sprinkled with the thyme leaves.

NOTES

celery

Coming into season in the fall, the long, ribbed stems of the celery plant are refreshingly crisp and may be white or green. The green version has been grown in full light, while the paler form has been cultivated covered by a light coating of earth to achieve a more delicate flavor.

Delicious cooked or raw, celery is an essential ingredient in most stocks and is good added to stews. Once cooked, the crunchy texture becomes soft and silky and the flavor mellows. Left raw, it can be sliced and added to salads, such as the famous apple and walnut Waldorf salad, or eaten simply as stalks. Celery stalks make the perfect tool for scooping up dips and are a great partner to those made with with cheese, particularly blue cheese (see below).

When buying, always look for firm, crisp heads and avoid any with blemishes, brown spots, or mushy patches. Celery should be used as soon as possible after buying, although it may be placed, root-end down, in a pitcher of cold water and stored in a cool place for several days.

To prepare celery, cut off the root, separate the head into stalks, and wash well to remove all traces of earth or grit. Celery is often "stringy," so strip out and pull off any strings as you trim off the root end. White celery tends to be stringier than green.

celery and blue cheese dip

By partnering this creamy, piquant blue cheese dip with crisp stalks of fresh celery—and perhaps a few handfuls of grapes—you will have a delicious appetizer that takes only minutes to prepare.

To make, simply crumble 7 ounces blue cheese (about 1½-2 cups) into a bowl and add ½ cup crème fraîche or sour cream. Season to taste with black pepper and beat thoroughly until really smooth and creamy. Chill in the fridge until ready to serve.

NOTES

Celery soup

SERVES 4

2 tbsp. butter
2 onions, finely chopped
2 tbsp. flour
3½ cups vegetable stock
1¼ lb. celery, trimmed
and sliced (about 6 cups)
1¾ cups milk
¼ cup crème fraîche or sour cream
salt and freshly ground black
pepper

Melt the butter in a pot and gently fry the onions for about 5 minutes. Stir in the flour and cook, stirring, for about 1 minute, then gradually stir in the stock.

Add the celery, bring to a boil, then reduce the heat, cover, and simmer gently for about 15 minutes.

Using a slotted spoon, remove about 3 large spoonfuls of celery and set aside. Pour the rest of the soup into a food processor or blender and blend until smooth.

Return the soup to the pot, add the reserved celery and the milk, and heat until just simmering. Remove from the heat, stir in the crème fraîche, season to taste, and serve.

Braised pheasant with celery

Celery, with its faintly salty flavor, is a classic partner for gamey pheasant and is wonderful cooked in white wine and served with a creamy sauce.

SERVES 4

2 tbsp. butter
2 pheasants, cleaned
3 strips of bacon, cut into small
pieces
1 cup chicken stock
1 cup white wine
1 lb. celery, trimmed and sliced
(about 4½ cups)
1 tbsp. cornstarch, blended with
1 tbsp. cold water
¼ cup crème fraîche or sour cream
large handful of fresh flat-leaf
parsley, roughly chopped
salt and freshly ground black pepper

Heat the oven to 350°F. Melt the butter in a large pan. Add the pheasants and brown all over, then transfer to a large flameproof and ovenproof pan, breast-side down. Scatter in the bacon pieces, pour in the stock and wine, cover, and cook in the oven for about 30 minutes. Turn over the pheasants and add the celery, tucking it in around the birds. Cover and cook for another 30 minutes, until the birds are cooked through.

Transfer the pheasants and celery to a serving dish and keep warm. Place the pan over a low heat, add the cornstarch paste to the cooking liquid and cook, stirring, until thickened. Stir in the crème fraîche and parsley, season to taste with salt and pepper, and transfer to a sauceboat or gravy boat to serve alongside the pheasant and celery.

fennel

Florence fennel, with its ridged greenish-white bulbs topped by a flourish of feathery fronds, was first cultivated in Italy in the 17th century. The crisp raw flesh is refreshingly juicy with a hint of anise. Fennel softens with cooking but still retains its distinctive flavor. Although good raw in salads—particularly when paired with juicy orange segments—it is also popular braised, steamed, roasted, or broiled and served as a vegetable. Add it to soups, coat in a creamy sauce, or smother with crème fraîche or another cream, sprinkle with Parmesan cheese and bake to make a mouthwatering gratin.

Buy small bulbs with a fresh white color, vibrant green leaves, and no blemishes or soft brown patches. It is usually necessary to remove the outer layer of flesh. Then slice the rest—either thinly for tossing into salads, or cut into thicker slices, halves, or quarters, ready for cooking.

Thin slices or chunks, brushed with olive oil and sprinkled with lemon juice and seasoning, make a wonderful addition to any summer barbecue.

Poussin (squab chicken) baked with fennel and vermouth

SERVES 4
juice of 1 lemon
2 cloves garlic, crushed
3 tbsp. olive oil
salt and freshly ground black pepper
2 squab chickens
3 heads of fennel
⅓ cup vermouth

Heat the oven to 375°F. Whisk together the lemon juice, garlic, and olive oil in small bowl, season to taste with salt and pepper, and set aside.

Season the chickens with salt and pepper and put in a roasting tin. Remove the green feathery fronds from the fennel and set aside. Slice the bulbs into quarters and arrange around the birds.

Pour the lemon and garlic mixture over the chickens and fennel and turn to coat all over. Grind a little pepper over them, then pour the vermouth over the fennel. Bake in the oven for about 45 minutes, spooning the juices over the birds and fennel from time to time, until the chickens are cooked and the fennel tender. The chickens are cooked if the juices run clear when a sharp knife is inserted into the thickest part of the thigh. Serve, garnished with the reserved fennel fronds, and the juices spooned over the top.

NOTES

mushrooms

Wild mushrooms have a much stronger flavor than the cultivated varieties and come in a vast array of shapes and sizes. Cèpes, also known as boletus or porcini, are probably the most prized of all wild mushrooms. They have fleshy pale-brown stalks and caps, and an intensely nutty taste. They can be dried by slicing, laying on a tray in a single layer, and placing in a warm place for several days. Once they have dried, store them in an airtight container; soak in hot water for about 30 minutes before using. Trumpet-shaped chanterelles are another highly valued mushroom, with an orangy hue and a distinctive, almost fruity, taste. They can also be dried and stored for later use. Blewits, with their bluish caps and lilac gills, are strikingly pretty and have a strong flavor that pairs well with similarly pungent ingredients such as onions and garlic. The large flat field mushroom, a close relative of the cultivated mushroom, is almost meaty in taste and texture.

As well as mushrooms, there are other edible wild fungi, the most lauded of all being the Piedmont or white truffle. Yellowish-brown with reddish mottled flesh and irregular in shape, these fungi grow underground and are so highly sought after that pigs and dogs are specially trained to hunt them out. They have a very distinctive, sweetly aromatic flavor and are usually finely sliced and cooked very quickly or shaved over a dish just before serving.

simple mushroom pâté

This richly flavored pâté makes a great appetizer or snack, served with crisp wafer-thin slices of toast. To make, melt a few pats of butter in a pan, toss in 2 chopped cloves of garlic and cook gently for a minute or two. Stir in about 1 pound of roughly chopped mixed mushrooms (about 4½–5½ cups), add a pinch of salt, and cook for another 10 minutes, until the juices start to run. Tip into a blender or food processor and blend briefly until finely chopped. Tranfer to a bowl, stir in cup of crème fraîche or sour cream, a handful of fine bread crumbs, and a handful of chopped fresh flat-leaf parsley. Season to taste with freshly grated nutmeg, lemon juice, salt, and freshly ground black pepper. Mix well and chill for at least an hour before serving.

NOTES

Wild mushroom soup

This rich, creamy soup, infused with aromatic sage, is perfect for serving as the weather begins to cool and you suddenly start to develop cravings for warming hearty food. Serve it piping hot, accompanied by chunks of warm, crusty bread, spread thickly with butter.

SERVES 4

¼ cup (½ stick) butter
1 onion, chopped
1 clove garlic, chopped
18 oz. mixed wild mushrooms, roughly chopped (about 5–6 cups)
1 tbsp. flour
½ cup white wine
4 cups vegetable stock
¼ cup crème fraîche or sour cream
handful of fresh sage leaves, chopped
2 tsp. chopped fresh flat-leaf parsley
salt and freshly ground black pepper

Melt the butter in a pot, add the onion and garlic and cook over a gentle heat for about 5 minutes, until soft. Add the mushrooms and cook for another 10 minutes.

Sprinkle the flour over the mushrooms and stir for about 1 minute. Gradually stir in the wine and stock and bring to a boil. Reduce the heat and let simmer for about 15 minutes.

Let it cool slightly, then tip the mushroom mixture into a food processor or blender and blend until smooth.

Pour into a clean pot and heat it through. Stir in the crème fraîche or sour cream and the chopped sage and parsley, season to taste with salt and pepper, and serve immedialely.

Wild mushroom pasta with spicy sausage

SERVES 4

6 spicy pork sausages
2 tbsp. olive oil
1 onion, finely chopped
2 cloves garlic, crushed
1¼ lb. mixed wild mushrooms, thickly sliced (about 6–7 cups)
salt and freshly ground black pepper
4 ripe plum tomatoes, peeled (see page 90), seeded, and chopped
2 tsp. chopped fresh sage
11 oz. spirals or shells pasta (about 4 cups)
freshly grated Parmesan cheese, for serving (optional)

Heat the broiler until hot. Arrange the sausages under the broiler and cook for about 5 minutes on each side, until well browned. Slice into ½-inch-thick chunks and set aside.

Heat the olive oil in large pan. Add the onion and garlic and cook gently for about 5 minutes, until soft. Add the mushrooms, sprinkle in a pinch of salt, and cook for about 10 minutes. Add the tomatoes, sage, and sausage chunks, and simmer gently for another 10 minutes, stirring now and again.

Meanwhile, cook the pasta in a pot of boiling salted water, according to the instructions on the package. Drain well.

Check the sauce for seasoning, then add the pasta and toss to combine. Serve immediately, sprinkled with a little Parmesan cheese, if you like.

Wild mushroom risotto *(opposite)*

SERVES 4

3 tbsp. vegetable oil
2 cloves garlic, finely chopped
18 oz. mixed wild mushrooms, sliced
(about 5-6 cups)
salt and freshly ground black pepper
about 5 cups vegetable stock
1 onion, finely chopped
1½ cups risotto rice
¾ cup white wine
handful of fresh chives, chopped,
plus extra for garnishing
1 cup grated Parmesan cheese, plus
shavings for serving

Heat half the oil in a large pan. Add half of the garlic and fry gently for about 1 minute. Add the mushrooms, sprinkle in a pinch of salt, and cook gently until the mushrooms start to release their juices. Increase the heat and cook, stirring occasionally, for about 5 minutes, until the juices have evaporated. Set aside. In a separate saucepan, bring the stock to a gentle simmer.

Heat the remaining oil in another large pan, then add the onion and remaining garlic, and fry gently for about 5 minutes. Add the risotto rice and cook, stirring, for 2 minutes. Add the wine and simmer, stirring, until nearly all the liquid has been absorbed. Add a ladleful of the hot stock and simmer, stirring, until nearly all the liquid has been absorbed. Add another ladleful of stock and continue cooking in this way for about 20 minutes, until the rice is tender but still has some bite. Just before the end of the cooking time, stir in the mushrooms.

Remove the pan from the heat, stir in the chopped chives and grated Parmesan cheese, and season to taste with black pepper. Serve sprinkled with Parmesan shavings and more chives.

Pork cooked with marsala and wild mushrooms

SERVES 4

2 tbsp. butter
4 pork loin chops, about
7 oz. each
2 cloves garlic, finely chopped
9 oz. mixed wild mushrooms, sliced
(about 2½-3 cups)
salt and freshly ground black pepper
¼ cup marsala or sherry
¼ tsp. fresh thyme leaves
2 tbsp. heavy cream

Melt the butter in a pan, add the pork chops, and brown for about 2-3 minutes on each side. Remove from the pan and set aside.

Add the garlic to the pan and fry gently for about 30 seconds, then add the mushrooms, sprinkle in a pinch of salt and cook for about 10 minutes until the juices have been released and have been slightly reduced.

Return the pork chops to the pan, pour in the marsala or sherry, stir in the thyme, and let it bubble gently for 5-6 minutes, until the meat is cooked through. Lift the chops onto warm serving plates. Stir the cream into the mushroom mixture, season with more salt, if needed, and pepper, spoon it over the chops, and serve.

NOTES

autumn squashes

Arriving in autumn (but known as "winter" squashes), cold-weather squashes are set apart from their summer cousins by their thick skins, orange or yellow flesh, and large, tough seeds. There are many different types. The pumpkin, with its dazzling orange skin, is widely available, as is the creamy, smooth-skinned butternut squash and the smaller acorn squash, with its fluted dark-green or bright-orange skin. Less common are the hubbard and the Asian kabocha squash.

With their sweet flavor and smooth texture, all squashes are delicious sautéed, roasted, baked, or steamed in their own juices, and can be added to stews, meat pies, and soups, used to stuff pasta, or tossed into salads. Their natural sweetness also makes them ideal for using in cakes and pies, pumpkin pie being the classic dessert served at Thanksgiving.

Buy only unblemished squashes that feel heavy for their size. Avoid really large ones, as they often lack flavor. To prepare, cut in half or into segments, then scoop out the seeds, which may then be roasted, cracked open, and eaten as a snack. If sautéeing or adding the squashes to a soup or stew, cut off the skin; if baking or roasting, you can remove the skin either before or after cooking.

Thai-style butternut squash curry

SERVES 4

2 cloves garlic, peeled
1-inch piece fresh ginger, peeled and grated
2 green chilies, seeded and chopped
3 shallots, chopped
4 kaffir lime leaves, shredded
2 lemongrass stalks, chopped
2 tbsp. sunflower oil
2½ cups vegetable stock
1⅓ cups cashews
1 tsp. Thai fish sauce
½ tsp. soft brown sugar
3 tbsp. creamed coconut
1½ butternut squashes, peeled, seeded, and sliced
juice of 1 lime
jasmine rice, for serving

Put the garlic, ginger, chilies, shallots, lime leaves, and lemongrass in a food processor or blender and blend to make a paste.

Heat the oil in a wok, add the paste, and fry for 1–2 minutes. Add the stock and bring to a boil. Reduce the heat and let simmer gently for about 10 minutes.

Meanwhile, heat a dry frying pan, add the cashews, and toast them, stirring, until golden, then remove from the pan.

Stir the fish sauce, sugar, and creamed coconut into the mixture in the wok, then add the butternut squash and cook for 8–10 minutes, until just tender. Stir in the cashews with lime juice to taste, and serve it with jasmine rice.

NOTES

Barley risotto with butternut squash

SERVES 4

2 butternut squashes, peeled,
seeded and cut into chunks
3 tbsp. olive oil
salt and freshly ground black pepper
1⅓ cups barley
1 onion, finely chopped
2 cloves garlic, finely chopped
⅓ cup white wine
½ cup vegetable stock
3 tbsp. crème fraîche or sour cream
4 fresh sage leaves, chopped
½ cup grated Parmesan cheese

Heat the oven to 400°F. Put the squashes in a roasting pan, drizzle about half the oil over it, tossing to coat, and season well with salt and pepper. Roast in the oven for about 30 minutes, turning once or twice during cooking, until tender.

Meanwhile, cook the barley in boiling water for about 25 minutes until tender. Drain and set aside.

Heat the remaining oil in a large pan, add the onion and garlic and fry gently for about 5 minutes, until soft. Stir in the drained barley, pour in the wine and stock, and let it bubble gently for about 5-10 minutes, stirring occasionally, until most of the liquid has been absorbed.

Stir in the crème fraîche, sage, and Parmesan cheese, then fold in the squashes. Season to taste with salt and pepper and serve.

Chicken tagine with roast squash

SERVES 4

2 cloves garlic, crushed
1-inch piece fresh ginger, peeled and
grated
2 tsp. harissa paste
juice of 1 lemon
3 tbsp. olive oil, plus extra
for brushing
salt and freshly ground black pepper
3-lb. chicken
7 oz. shallots, peeled (about 2 cups)
2 tsp. honey
1 cup water
1 tsp. ground cinnamon
1 butternut squash, about
1½ lb. in weight, peeled, seeded, and
cut into thick slices

Combine the garlic, ginger, harissa, lemon juice, and 1 tablespoon of the olive oil, and season well with salt and pepper. Pour this all over the chicken—inside and out—cover and let marinate for at least 1 hour.

Heat the remaining oil in a heavy pan or tagine, add the shallots, and cook over a low heat, stirring frequently, for 10 minutes. Add the honey and about 1½ tablespoons of the water and season to taste with salt and pepper. Cook for 5 minutes, until sticky and golden. Push the shallots to the side of the pan and add the chicken. Sprinkle in the cinnamon, pour in the marinating juices and the rest of the water, and bring to a boil. Reduce the heat, cover, and simmer for 1 hour, turning the chicken occasionally, until cooked through.

Meanwhile, heat the oven to 400°F. Twenty minutes before the chicken is ready, put the squash in a baking pan, brush with oil, season well, and roast in the oven for 20 minutes.

Remove the chicken from the pan and keep warm. If the sauce is very liquid, boil rapidly for about 5 minutes to thicken. Arrange the squash around the chicken. Pour the sauce over and serve.

Pumpkin gnocchi with sage butter

SERVES 4

9 oz. prepared pumpkin flesh, cut into chunks (about 2 cups)
1 tbsp. olive oil
1¼ lb. potatoes, boiled
2 egg yolks
1 heaping cup all-purpose flour
pinch of salt
pinch of freshly grated nutmeg
pinch of ground cinnamon
salt

FOR THE SAGE BUTTER
¼ cup (½ stick) butter
8 fresh sage leaves

Heat the oven to 400°F. Put the pumpkin in a baking dish, drizzle the oil over it, and toss to coat, then bake in the oven for about 20 minutes, until tender. Mash the potatoes and cooked pumpkin together in a large bowl, then push through a strainer and stir in the egg yolks.

Combine the flour, salt, nutmeg, and cinnamon in another bowl, then gradually work into the pumpkin mixture to form a soft dough. To form the gnocchi, divide the dough into four, then gently roll each piece into a long sausage, about ½-inch in diameter. Cut each length of dough into 1-inch-long pieces and press each lightly with a fork to make an indent on one side and a ridged pattern on the other. Set aside on a sheet of waxed paper.

Make the sage butter. Heat the butter in a pan until sizzling, then add the sage leaves and cook for about 1 minute until the leaves are crisp. Keep warm.

Bring a large pot of salted water to a boil, then add the gnocchi and cook for 2-3 minutes, until they rise to the surface. Scoop them out using a slotted spoon, drain well, and serve immediately, drizzled with the sage butter.

spiced pumpkin soup

To make this wonderfully warming soup, cut a pumpkin, about 3 pounds in weight, into wedges, scoop out the seeds, and arrange the pumpkin in a roasting pan. Drizzle a few tablespoons of olive oil over it, season well with salt and freshly ground black pepper, and roast in a heated oven at 400°F for about 30 minutes, until tender. Meanwhile, heat another tablespoon of oil in a large pot, add 2 chopped onions and 2 crushed garlic cloves, and cook gently until soft. Sprinkle in 1 teaspoon of ground cinnamon and 1 tablespoon of chopped preserved lemon (or, if unavailable, the grated zest of 1 lemon), then pour in about 5 cups of vegetable or chicken stock and bring to a boil. Reduce the heat and let simmer for 10 minutes. Scoop the pumpkin out of its skin and toss it into the pot along with 2 teaspoons of harissa. Pour into a blender or food processor and blend until really smooth. Heat through, check the seasoning, and serve.

NOTES

sweet potatoes

Sweet potatoes come into season in the fall and last right through the winter. They may have brown, creamy-yellow, or red skins, with flesh varying from pale cream to a deep orange that becomes soft and smooth with a sweet nutty flavor when cooked. Introduced to Europe from the Americas in 1493, and cultivated in southern Spain from the early 16th century, they have had many moments of culinary popularity. They grow best in warmer climates and can be grown successfully in cooler regions only when started off under glass.

When buying, choose smooth-skinned potatoes of an even size and shape. Avoid any that are soft, damaged, or beginning to sprout. They keep well if stored in a cool dark place, preferably in an airy basket or similar container. To prepare, scrub them well, then cook in the same way as ordinary potatoes—steam, boil, mash, sauté, roast, or deep-fry. When boiled, they are best cooked in their skins, then peeled, to preserve their taste and texture. They are also wonderful baked and stuffed with a piquant filling, such as blue cheese or hot beef chili and sour cream, to offset their sweet buttery flesh.

Sweet potato and chicken curry (opposite)

SERVES 4

2 tbsp. sunflower oil
8 green cardamom pods, split open
1 onion, finely chopped
2 cloves garlic, finely chopped
1-inch piece fresh ginger, peeled and grated
2 green chilies, seeded and chopped
½ tsp. turmeric
2 tsp. ground coriander seed
1¾ cups coconut milk
salt
8 chicken thighs, skinned
1½ lb. sweet potatoes, peeled and cut into large chunks
juice of 1 lemon
small handful of fresh cilantro leaves
rice or Indian breads, for serving

Heat the oil in a large pot. Add the cardamom pods and fry over medium heat for about 2 minutes. Add the onion, garlic, ginger, and chilies, and fry gently, stirring, for about 5 minutes.

Stir in the turmeric, ground coriander seed, and coconut milk, season to taste with salt, and bring to a boil. Add the chicken thighs, pressing them down into the sauce, reduce the heat, and let simmer for 5 minutes. Stir in the sweet potatoes, cover, and continue to simmer for another 10 minutes.

Uncover the pot, increase the heat slightly, and cook for about 10 minutes more, until the chicken is cooked through, the sauce has thickened, and the sweet potatoes are tender. Stir once or twice towards the end of the cooking time to prevent the sauce from sticking to the bottom of the pan. Stir in lemon juice to taste and serve, sprinkled with the fresh cilantro leaves and accompanied by rice or Indian breads.

NOTES

citrus fruits

Most citrus fruits thrive in warmer Mediterranean climates, although the tropical lime needs hotter weather to grow successfully. Different citrus fruits come into season at different times of the year, with some, such as Valencia oranges, being available at almost any time and others, such as naval and blood oranges, lemons, limes, and grapefruits, being most abundant in autumn and winter.

The sweeter fruits such as oranges, tangerines, clementines, kumquats, and grapefruits, along with hybrids, such as ugli fruit and mineolas, can be eaten on their own, while limes and lemons, with their sour juice, work best as flavorings. Citrus segments can be delicious tossed into salads—bittersweet grapefruit is good paired with avocado and crispy bacon, while oranges are delicious with anise-like fennel or sweet beets. Orange juice is a popular additon to many Mediterranean savory dishes (for example, in pork stews or fish dishes), while lemons and limes feature constantly in marinades. Astringent lemon or lime juice is also used to "pickle" uncooked fish in dishes such as gravadlax and seviche.

Buy firm fruits that feel heavy for their size, as this indicates plenty of juice. If the rind or zest is needed in a recipe, use unwaxed fruits. Many fruits, such as oranges and clementines, can simply be peeled and eaten as they are. Grapefruit is often cut in half, the segments cut away from the membranes with a special curved knife, and served in their shell. To prepare orange or grapefruit segments without their membranes for a salad, cut a slice off the top and bottom of the fruit to reveal the flesh. Then, with a sharp knife, cut off the skin, with the white pith and membrane, around the whole fruit in strips. Hold the fruit over a bowl to catch any juice, then slice down between the membranes dividing the individual segments to release the flesh.

zesty lemon curd

This is delicious spread on buttered bread or English muffins, but is equally good stirred into crème fraîche or whipped cream to make a rich citrus cream. It is also wonderful spooned onto pancakes or used to line the bottom of fresh-fruit tarts.

To make about 1 pound, put the grated rind and juice of 3 large lemons into the top of a double boiler over simmering water, so that the bottom of the top pan does not touch the water. Add 1 cup of sugar and stir until the sugar has dissolved. Roughly chop ½ cup (1 stick) of unsalted butter into small chunks and stir in until melted. Through a fine mesh strainer, pour 3 large beaten eggs and continue cooking, stirring constantly, until the mixture thickens and coats the back of the spoon. Pour into sterilized jars and seal. Let cool, then label and store in the fridge. Use within 3 months.

NOTES

Orange and beet salad

The sharp acidity of oranges makes them the perfect partner for sweet tender beets, creating a vibrantly colored salad that really livens up the autumn table.

SERVES 4

11 oz. cooked beets
(about 2-2½ cups)
2 oranges
¼ red onion, thinly sliced
¼ cup walnut halves
2 tsp. red wine vinegar
¼ tsp. Dijon mustard
2 tbsp. olive oil
salt and freshly ground black pepper

Slice the beets and place in a serving bowl. Using a sharp knife, slice off the top and bottom of each orange down to the flesh, then, holding it over a clean bowl, slice off in downward strips the peel, white pith, and membrane, right down to the flesh. Slice along the membranes between the segments to release the flesh. Discard the peel, pith, and membranes and reserve the juice in the bowl. Add the segments to the beets, then toss in the onion and walnuts.

Make a dressing by whisking together the reserved orange juice, the vinegar, and mustard, then whisk in the oil and season with salt and pepper to taste. Drizzle it over the salad, toss gently to combine, and serve.

Pork cooked with orange and white beans

SERVES 4

2 tbsp. olive oil
1 onion, finely chopped
2 cloves garlic, crushed
18 oz. pork loin, trimmed
and cubed (about 2¼ cups)
4 oz. chorizo, cut into
small chunks (about 1 cup)
2 tsp. ground cumin
2 tsp. ground coriander seed
grated rind and juice of 1 orange
18 oz. tomatoes, peeled (see page
90), seeded, and chopped
(about 2 cups)
salt and freshly ground black pepper
15-oz. can Great Northern beans,
drained and rinsed
juice of ½ lemon

Heat the oil in a pan, add the onion and garlic, and fry gently for about 5 minutes, until soft. Add the pork and chorizo, sprinkle in the ground cumin and coriander seed, and cook, stirring, for about 1-2 minutes.

Add the orange rind and juice and the tomatoes, then season to taste with salt and pepper and stir to mix in. Bring to a boil, lower the heat, and let simmer gently for about 45 minutes, stirring once or twice, until the sauce becomes thick.

Stir in the drained beans and let simmer for another 10 minutes. Season again with more salt and pepper if necessary, then add lemon juice to taste. Serve.

NOTES

Orange and ginger steamed pudding

Infused with the flavors of orange and warming ginger, this indulgent dessert is perfect for bringing a cheering glow to the table during the colder months. To enjoy it to the full, serve with a generous helping of whipped cream.

SERVES 6

½ cup (1 stick) butter, at room temperature
½ cup sugar
2 eggs
grated rind and juice of 1 orange
3 pieces preserved ginger in syrup, chopped
¾ cup plus 2 tbsp. all-purpose flour
1½ tsp. baking powder
½ tsp. salt
whipped cream, for serving

FOR THE SAUCE

finely pared rind of 1 orange
¼ cup sugar
2 tbsp. syrup from the preserved ginger jar
2 tbsp. corn syrup

Grease a 5-cup pudding mold. Make the sauce by putting the orange rind in a pan of boiling water, lowering the heat, and letting it simmer for about 4 minutes. Drain well, pat dry with paper towels, and set aside. Put the sugar in a clean pan and heat very gently, stirring, for about 4 minutes, until it melts and turns pale gold. Remove from the heat, then stir in the orange rind, followed by the ginger syrup and corn syrup. Pour the sauce into the greased pudding mold and set aside.

In a large mixing bowl, beat together the butter and sugar until pale and fluffy. Beat in the eggs, one at a time, then stir in the orange rind and juice and the chopped ginger. Sift the flour over the top and carefully fold in.

Tip the batter mixture on top of the sauce in the pudding mold, spreading it out in an even layer. Cover the mold with a double layer of foil and tie it securely in place with string. Put a poaching ring or jam-jar lid in the bottom of a large pan and place the mold on top. Pour water into the pan to come about two thirds of the way up the side of the mold. Bring the water to a boil, then reduce the heat, cover the pan, and let simmer gently for about 1½ hours. Check the water level now and again to make sure it is high enough and add more if necessary.

Carefully remove the mold from the pan and let rest for about 5 minutes before removing the foil and turning the pudding out onto a serving plate. Serve hot with cream.

Lemon tart *(opposite)*

Few desserts can equal a good lemon tart for indulgence and sophistication. The tang of fresh lemon gives a mouth-puckering lift to the rich creamy sweetness. This version pairs a crisp almond crust with a really zesty filling.

SERVES 6-8

¾ cup crème fraîche or sour cream
4 eggs
grated rind of 2 lemons
juice of 5 lemons
¾ cup sugar, plus about
2-3 tbsp. for the topping

FOR THE PIE CRUST
⅔ cup all-purpose flour
2 tsp. caster sugar
½ cup ground almonds
¼ cup (½ stick) butter, chilled and cubed
about 1 tbsp. cold water

First make the pie dough. Put the flour, sugar, and almonds in a food processor and pulse to combine. Add the butter and blend until the mixture resembles fine bread crumbs. With the machine running, add just enough water for the mixture to come together in a ball. Press the dough together, wrap in plastic wrap, and leave in the fridge to chill for at least 30 minutes.

Heat the oven to 400°F. Roll out the dough to line a greased 8-inch pie plate, cover with foil, and scatter in some baking beans. Bake in the oven for about 10 minutes. Remove the foil and beans and cook for another 5-10 minutes until the bottom is crisp. Remove the pie shell from the oven and reduce the temperature to 325°C.

Meanwhile, put the crème fraîche in a bowl and beat in the eggs, one at a time, then stir in the lemon rind and juice and sugar. Pour the mixture into the pie shell, then return it to the oven and bake for 30-35 minutes, until the filling is just set but is still wobbly.

Let cool for about 20 minutes, then sprinkle with a thin layer of sugar and heat with a kitchen blow-torch until the top is browned and bubbling. Alternatively, cover the pie crust edges with foil and place the tart under a hot broiler until the sugar is browned and bubbling.

NOTES

grapes

The grape harvest comes at the beginning of autumn, after the long weeks of summer sunshine that are needed to ripen the succulent flesh. The flavor can vary from sugary or tart to the rich scented sweetness of the muscat grape. The skins range in color from pale yellow through green and red to a dark bluish-black, depending on the variety. Some grapes also have a dusky bloom, while others are waxy.

There are many different types of grape, some grown for eating, others exclusively for making into wine or drying into raisins, golden raisins, and currants. Many contain tiny seeds, but there are also a number of seedless varieties. Dessert grapes are delicious simply eaten on their own, snipped straight from the bunch using a pair of scissors. However, they can also be paired with a multitude of other ingredients. They have a particular affinity with cheese, so serve alongside a cheeseboard or cut in half on top of an open cheese sandwhich. They can also be made into juices, sherbets, and jellies, used in tarts and cakes, and in savory dishes. Cook them with poultry and feathered game or add to soups.

When buying grapes, the easiest way to check that the fruit is ripe and has a good flavor is to taste a loose fallen grape, if at all possible. Avoid any that are soft, wrinkled, blemished, or showing traces of browning or mold. Heavy use of chemicals is frequent in grape cultivation, so it is particularly important to wash the fruits before eating. Rinse them well, then place on a clean cloth to dry. Peeled grapes are often called for in recipes. To peel them, put the grapes in a heatproof bowl, cover with boiling water, then drain almost immediately. The skins should then peel away easily. If the skins still cling to the fruit, repeat the process and try again. To seed grapes, slice in half, then simply pick out the seeds using the point of a sharp knife.

NOTES

Almond and grape soup

SERVES 4

1 cup blanched almonds
7 oz. day-old white bread, crusts removed
1 clove garlic, chopped
5 tbsp. olive oil
1½ cups whole seedless grapes, plus a handful, sliced
about 2 cups vegetable stock
salt and freshly ground black pepper
1 tbsp. sherry vinegar or white wine vinegar
2 tbsp. sherry

Heat a dry frying pan, add the almonds, and toast them for about 5 minutes until lightly browned. Tip into a food processor or blender and blend until finely ground. Leave in the food processor or blender.

Soak the bread in 1¼ cups cold water for about 10 minutes, then squeeze dry. Add to the ground almonds, along with the garlic, and blend to form a paste.

With the motor running, gradually add the oil and whole grapes, then add enough stock to make a smooth soup. Season to taste with salt and pepper, and stir in the vinegar and sherry. Pour into a bowl and chill in the fridge for at least 2 hours. Serve, with the sliced grapes stirred in.

Rare beef salad with grapes and wasabi dressing

SERVES 4

9 oz. beef sirloin
olive oil, for brushing
juice of 1 lime
¼–½ tsp. wasabi paste
2 tbsp. sunflower oil
handful of fresh cilantro, chopped
salt
2 large handfuls mixed salad greens, such as lettuce, arugula, baby spinach, and chicory
1½ cups seedless grapes, cut in half

Trim any fat or sinew from the meat and brush with olive oil. Heat a grill pan or broiler until very hot, then cook the meat for about 2 minutes on each side, or to your taste. Lift onto a board, cover with foil, and let rest for 10 minutes.

Meanwhile, make a dressing by stirring together the lime juice and wasabi paste, then whisking in the sunflower oil and chopped cilantro. Season to taste with salt and set aside.

Divide the salad greens between four serving bowls, then sprinkle the grapes on top. Slice the meat thinly and scatter it over the salads. Pour the dressing on top, toss to combine, and serve.

NOTES

Walnut scones with Brie and grapes

Sweet juicy grapes have a natural affinity with cheese and are fabulous served on top of these savory scones for afternoon tea or a simple snack (scones are just like biscuits). Mild creamy Brie is suggested here, but almost any type of cheese will work well. Try a piquant blue cheese or a sharp Cheddar.

MAKES 12

1⅔ cups self-rising flour, plus extra
for dusting
1 tsp. baking powder
pinch of cayenne pepper
pinch of salt
¼ cup (½ stick) unsalted butter,
chilled and cubed
½ cup walnut pieces
1 egg, beaten
½ cup milk

FOR SERVING

about 6 oz. Brie cheese
(about 1½ cups)
about 1½ cups seedless grapes,
sliced

Heat the oven to 425°C. Grease a baking sheet.

Combine the flour, baking powder, cayenne pepper, and salt in a large bowl. Add the butter and rub into the flour, using your fingertips, until the mixture resembles fine bread crumbs. Stir in the walnuts and make a well in the center.

Beat the egg and milk together in a small bowl. Reserving about 1½ tablespoons of the mixture, pour the rest into the well in the flour mixture and gradually bring together using a fork to form a soft dough. Add extra milk, if necessary. Turn out onto a lightly floured surface and knead very briefly, then roll out to about an inch thick. Using a 2-inch biscuit cutter, cut the dough into 12 circles. Arrange on the baking sheet, spacing them slightly apart. Brush the tops with the reserved milk and egg mixture and bake for about 10 minutes, until risen and golden. Transfer to a wire rack to cool.

To serve, split the cooled scones in half horizontally and top each half with a slice of Brie and a scattering of sliced grapes.

grape jelly

Grape jelly is delicious spread on toast. This version is scented with cardamom, but fresh ginger or elderflower syrup both work well, too. Put 2 pounds of grapes (about 6 cups) in a pan with the juice and seeds of 2 lemons and the crushed seeds of about 10 cardamom pods. Bring to a boil, reduce the heat, cover, and simmer for about 1½ hours. Mash the grapes with a potato masher, then pour the mixture into a scalded jelly bag suspended over a large glass bowl and let it drain overnight. Never squeeze the bag as this will give cloudy results. Measure the juice collected into a clean pan and add 1 pound of sugar for every 2½ cups of grape juice. Heat gently, stirring, until the sugar has dissolved, then bring to a boil and cook until the jelly reaches 220°F. Skim off any scum, then ladle into sterilized jars and cover, seal, and label. Store in a cool, dark place.

figs

The appearance of figs marks the closing days of summer and the start of the fall. Figs thrive in warm climates and have been cultivated in the Mediterranean and Middle East for millennia. Depending on variety, they may have green, amber, or purplish-black skin, the tender insides being made up almost entirely of tiny dark seeds, surrounded by pink, amber, violet, and red flesh.

When figs are really fresh and ripe, they are wonderful eaten just as they are. Simply cut in half and scoop out the tasty flesh with a teaspoon. They are also delicious cut into wedges and tossed into salads, or try scooping fresh fig flesh on top of prosciutto or blue cheese in a sandwich instead of a classic chutney. Figs are also good cooked—in fruit compotes or a sweet syrup, in tarts, in jams and preserves, and dished up with game or poultry.

When choosing figs, look for plump, unblemished fruits that give slightly when gently squeezed. They need little preparation apart from washing. Cut or slice them lengthwise so that you can still appreciate the shape of the whole fruit. Raw figs are best eaten warm, never cold or chilled. If you can, place them on a sunny windowsill for an hour or so before serving.

baked figs with honey and crème fraîche

One of the best and simplest ways to eat figs is to bake them with honey and crème fraîche to make a glorious melt-in-the-mouth dessert. Allow about 3 figs per person. Trim off the woody tip of each fig and cut halfway down each one into quarters, then gently press the bottom so that the quarters splay out. Arrange the figs in a baking dish, spoon about a tablespoon of crème fraîche (or sour cream) into each one, then drizzle a little honey on top. Bake in a heated oven at 425°F for 5-10 minutes until golden and bubbling. Serve immediately with the syrupy juices spooned on top.

NOTES

Guinea fowl cooked with figs and red wine

SERVES 6

2 guinea fowl, about
2¼ lb. each
salt and freshly ground black pepper
3 tbsp. olive oil
8 figs, cut in half
large handful of fresh thyme
1 cup red wine
1 cup chicken stock
1 tbsp. flour

Heat the oven to 350°F. Season the birds all over with plenty of salt and pepper. Heat 2 tablespoons of the oil in a large frying pan, add the birds, and brown on all sides. Transfer to a baking dish or roasting pan.

Arrange the figs around the birds, tuck in the sprigs of thyme and pour in the wine and stock. Roast in the oven for about 1 hour, until the juices run clear when the thickest part of the thigh is pierced with a knife or skewer.

Remove the birds and figs from the dish, cover with foil, and keep warm. Discard the thyme. Heat the remaining oil in a pan and stir in the flour. Cook for about 1 minute, then stir in the cooking juices and heat gently until thickened to a rich gravy. Transfer to a sauceboat or gravy boat and serve with the guinea fowl and figs.

Fig and goat cheese salad

SERVES 4

1 tbsp. balsamic vinegar
2 tbsp. olive oil
salt and freshly ground black pepper
1½ tbsp. pine nuts
about 3 large handfuls salad greens,
such as lettuce, arugula, baby
spinach, and chicory
4 figs, cut into wedges
8 slices of a baguette
7 oz. goat cheese, cut into
8 slices (about 1½-2 cups)
2 tsp. honey

Make a dressing by whisking together the vinegar and oil in a small bowl. Season to taste with salt and pepper and set aside.

Heat a dry frying pan, add the pine nuts and toast them, stirring, for about 3 minutes until golden. Set aside. Divide the salad greens between four serving plates and scatter the fig wedges on top.

Heat the broiler until hot and toast the bread on one side only until golden. Turn over, place a slice of cheese on each piece of bread, then drizzle with honey and a grinding of black pepper. Broil for 2-3 minutes, until golden and bubbling.

Drizzle the dressing over each salad, top each with two cheesy toasts, sprinkle with the pine nuts, and serve immediately.

NOTES

Roast fig tartlets

These simple-to-make little tartlets are fabulous eaten warm or at room temperature. The subtle combination of the crisp almond crust, mild vanilla custard, and sweet, fragrant figs is absolutely irresistible. You will find it hard to stop at just one.

MAKES 12
⅓ cup crème fraîche or sour cream
1 egg yolk
¼ tsp. vanilla extract
½ tbsp. confectioners' sugar
6 figs
½-1 tbsp. clear honey

FOR THE PIE CRUST
3 tbsp. ground almonds
¾ cup all-purpose flour
1 tbsp. sugar
¼ cup (½ stick) butter, chilled and cubed
2 tbsp. water

First make the pie dough. Put the almonds, flour, and sugar in a food processor and pulse to combine. Add the butter and pulse until the mixture resembles fine bread crumbs. With the motor running, gradually add the water until the mixture comes together in a ball. Wrap in plastic wrap and chill in the fridge for at least 30 minutes.

Heat the oven to 375°F and grease a 12-cup muffin pan. Roll out the dough thinly. Cut out 12 circles, using a 3-inch round biscuit cutter. Press the circles into the muffin pan and prick the bottoms with a fork. Bake for about 10 minutes in the oven until crisp and lightly golden.

Meanwhile, beat together the crème fraîche, egg yolk, vanilla extract, and confectioners' sugar in a bowl and set aside. Cut off the woody tip from the stem of each fig, then cut the fruits in half lengthwise.

Remove the mini tart shells from the oven and put a tablespoon of the crème fraîche mixture in the bottom of each. Nestle a fig half on top and add a little more of the crème fraîche mixture if there's room. Drizzle with honey and bake in the oven for about 10 minutes, until the figs are tender and the custard is just turning golden. Remove to a wire rack to cool slightly before serving.

cheese, ham, and fig croissant

Figs, partnered with melting cheese and prosciutto, make a sublime filling for a toasted croissant. Cut the croissant in half and top the bottom half with a slice of Gruyère (or Swiss) cheese. Lightly toast both halves until the cheese on one is melting and the other is golden. Top the cheesy half with a couple of slices of prosciutto and a few scoops of flesh from a ripe fig. Grind some black pepper over it, place the toasted half-croissant on top, and enjoy.

pomegranates

Native to Iran, pomegranates thrive in hot sunny climates. They arrive on our tables in late autumn. Round, tapering to an elegant, chimney-like stem, these leathery-skinned fruit are tightly packed with glistening, jewel-like, red seeds, each rich with an intensely flavored sweet-sour juice, which can be used in both sweet and savory dishes—much in the same way that lemon juice is. This juice is particularly popular in Persian cuisine and is also made into a sweet concentrated syrup called grenadine, that can be added to cocktails and be diluted with water to make a refreshing drink. As they are so attractive, the whole seeds are frequently sprinkled over dishes as a garnish.

When buying pomegranates, choose fruit that feel heavy for their size, as this indicates that they contain plenty of juice. To remove the seeds, cut the fruit into quarters and, holding each piece over a bowl, sharply tap the back with a wooden spoon. The seeds should pop out unscathed into the bowl and can then be used whole or pressed in a strainer to extract the juice.

Pan-fried duck with pomegranate sauce (opposite)

SERVES 4
4 ripe pomegranates
4 duck breasts, about 7 oz. each
salt and freshly ground black pepper
2 cloves garlic, crushed
1 tbsp. flour
½ cup chicken or duck stock

Cut the pomegranates into quarters, hold each piece over a bowl, and tap the back sharply with a wooden spoon, so that the seeds pop out. Set about a quarter of them aside. Put the rest in a strainer over a clean bowl and press with the back of a spoon to release the juice.

Score the skin of the duck in a lattice pattern and rub with plenty of salt and pepper. Heat a nonstick frying pan and place the duck, skin-side down, in the pan. Cook for 10 minutes over medium heat. Pour away most of the fat, then turn the duck over and cook for another 4–5 minutes. Remove from the pan, set aside, and keep warm.

Add the garlic to the pan and stir for about 30 seconds, then stir in the flour and continue stirring, for 1 minute. Gradually stir in the pomegranate juice and stock and cook for 2–3 minutes, until the sauce has thickened. Season to taste with salt and pepper, then stir in the reserved pomegranate seeds. Serve with the duck.

NOTES

plums

Glorious fat plums with their bluish bloom help welcome in the fall. There are hundreds of different varieties—including damsons and greengages—and their skin-color ranges from dark purple to red, green, and yellow. All have fragrant juicy flesh, that can vary from pinkish red to golden amber. Dessert plums can be eaten raw or cooked—baked, poached, or even pan-fried with sugar, or in pies and cakes. The cooking plums are tarter with a drier flesh and are good for poaching, baking, and making into jam. Golden-skinned greengages have a honeyed taste and are particularly good eaten raw, while blue-black damsons have an intense tart flavor, making them better suited to cooking.

When buying, look for firm, unblemished fruits. A good blue-purplish bloom indicates that they have not been overhandled. Plums should be eaten within a few days, as they become too soft and become over-ripe very quickly.

Plums may be cooked with the pit in or out. To remove it, cut around the plum along its natural crease, then gently twist the two sides apart and pry out the pit. When making a puree, simply cook the plums whole, then strain out the pits and skin. When making jam, just skim the pits off the surface during cooking.

If skinned plums are called for in a recipe, cut a cross in the bottom of each fruit, place in a heatproof bowl, and cover with boiling water. Let them stand for about 30 seconds, then drain. The skins should peel away easily.

oven-poached plums

Plums are wonderful poached, then served hot or cold with plenty of cream or crème fraîche. To prepare, heat the oven to 300°F. Arrange 18 ounces plums (about 2½–3 cups), cut in half and pitted in a single layer in a large baking dish. Sprinkle a little ground cinnamon and 1 tablespoon of sugar over them. Tuck in 3 whole cloves around the fruit, pour in the juice of 1 orange and 1 tablespoon of brandy, then bake in the oven for about 30 minutes, spooning the juices over the plums once or twice during cooking.

NOTES

Plum and marzipan tarte tatin

The classic *tarte tatin* is made with apples. This version, however—made with marzipan-stuffed plums—makes a wonderful alternative. You can also use the basic recipe for an apple or pear tart if you wish: just peel, cut in half, and core the fruit, toss in lemon juice, and cook as described below, omitting the marzipan.

SERVES 6-8

14 oz. puff pastry dough
flour, for dusting
⅓ cup marzipan
¼ cup (½ stick) butter
¼ cup sugar
1¼ lb. plums, cut in half and pitted (about 3-3½ cups)
crème fraîche or sour cream, for serving

Heat the oven to 400°F. Roll out the dough on a lightly floured surface and, using a round 9-inch-wide pan as a guide, cut out a large circle. Roll it up, wrap in plastic wrap, and set aside in the refrigerator.

Divide the marzipan into 16-20 pieces (according the number of plum halves you have), roll into balls, and flatten slightly so that they will fit into the plums. Set aside.

Melt the butter in a cast iron frying pan and sprinkle in the sugar. Let it bubble for 1-2 minutes, then arrange the plums, cut-side up, in a single layer in the pan and let it bubble for another 8-9 minutes, until the syrup is dark and caramely.

Remove the pan from the heat and place a flattened ball of marzipan in the center of each plum half. Place the circle of pastry dough over the top of the fruit, tucking the edges down around the plums. Bake in the oven for 25-30 minutes until the crust is puffed up and golden.

Let the tart cool for about 10 minutes, then place a serving plate over the top of the pan and carefully flip it over to tip the tart out of the pan on to the plate, so the fruit is now on top. If necessary, rearrange the fruit slightly. Serve warm or at room temperature with a generous helping of crème fraîche or sour cream.

NOTES

apples

There are thousands of different varieties of apple, coming into season at different times. Many keep well, so apples are usually available from cold-storage and can be enjoyed for most of the year. Early-cropping apples, however—coming in at the end of summer and beginning of autumn—tend not to store well, so should be taken advantage of while in season.

As a general rule, apples can be split into two groups: "eating" and "cooking." Eating apples are sweet and good eaten raw, although they may be cooked, while cooking apples are sour and are usually prepared with sugar.

Choose firm, unblemished apples and avoid those that are wrinkled or bruised. Remember that skin color is no indication of flavor. To prepare for cooking, simply peel and core. Apple flesh quickly turns brown when exposed to air so, unless using the fruit immediately, toss cut apples in lemon juice to preserve their crisp creamy color.

Apples are delicious cooked in tarts, pies, cakes, and other desserts, and go well with warm spices such as cinnamon, ginger, and cloves. Stew them in a splash of water with a couple of whole cloves, or bake them in a crumble. Cooking apples can be cored, then stuffed with sugar, dried fruit, and butter, and baked until tender, or turned into a sharp sauce to serve with pork.

Spicy pork chops with caramelized apples

SERVES 4
2 tart cooking apples
2 tbsp. butter
1 tsp. soft brown sugar
2 tsp. balsamic vinegar
salt and freshly ground black pepper
1 tbsp. olive oil
4 pork loin steaks, about 7 oz. each
¼ cup sherry
6 juniper berries, crushed

Peel, core, and quarter the apples. Melt the butter in a frying pan, add the prepared apples, and fry for about 3 minutes, turning to cook all over. Sprinkle in the sugar and vinegar and season to taste with salt and pepper. Cook, turning occasionally, for about 5 minutes, until caramelized and sticky. Set aside.

Heat the oil in a clean frying pan, add the pork steaks, and cook for about 3 minutes on each side, until well browned. Add the sherry, juniper berries, and caramelized apples. Season to taste with more salt and pepper, if needed, and let it bubble gently for about 5-6 minutes, until the pork is cooked through. Serve.

NOTES

Apple strudel

SERVES 6-8

1 tsp. ground cinnamon
1 tbsp. soft brown sugar
½ cup blanched almonds
½ cup golden raisins
2 large eating apples
12 sheets phyllo dough
melted butter, for brushing
confectioners' sugar, for dusting

Heat the oven to 375°F. Grease a baking sheet.

Combine the cinnamon and sugar in a large bowl and set aside. Heat a dry frying pan, add the almonds, and toast them for 3 minutes, stirring, until golden. Roughly chop, and add to the sugar and cinnamon mixture along with the raisins. Peel, core, and slice the apples, then add to the mixture and toss together to combine.

Lay one sheet of phyllo dough on a board, brush with melted butter, then lay another sheet next to it, overlapping slightly, and again brush it with melted butter. Add a third overlapping sheet to make a large rectangle and brush that with butter. Lay another three sheets on top, arranging and buttering them in the same way. Repeat with the remaining phyllo sheets until there are four layers of dough.

Spread the apple mixture down the center of the pastry dough, leaving space at either end. Tuck the short ends of the pastry over the apple filling, then roll up into a log. Carefully lift onto the baking sheet, tucking the folded ends underneath. Brush with more melted butter, then bake in the oven for about 35 minutes, until crisp and golden. Serve warm or cold, dusted with confectioners' sugar.

Brandied baked apples

SERVES 4

4 tart cooking apples
¼ cup (½ stick) butter, at room temperature
2 tbsp. brown sugar
handful of ready-to-eat dried figs, finely chopped
handful of ready-to-eat dried apricots, finely chopped
1 tsp. ground cinnamon
juice of 2 oranges
5 tbsp. brandy
thick cream, for serving

Heat the oven to 375°F. Core the apples, leaving them whole, and place in a baking dish.

Cream together the butter and brown sugar, then stir in the dried figs, apricots, and the cinnamon. Using a teaspoon, fill the cored apples with the mixture.

Pour the orange juice and brandy over the apples, cover the dish with foil, and bake in the oven for 35 minutes. Remove the foil and cook for about 15 minutes more, until the apples are tender. Serve with the juices drizzled over the top and a generous helping of thick cream.

NOTES

Apple and blackberry crumble

SERVES 4-6
4 eating apples
1 cup blackberries
2 tsp. ground cinnamon
thick cream or custard, for serving

FOR THE CRUMBLE
¾ cup flour
½ cup (1 stick) chilled butter, chopped
¼ cup soft brown sugar
¾ cup hazelnuts, toasted and roughly chopped

Heat the oven to 375°F. First make the crumble. Put the flour, butter, and sugar in a food processor and process until the mixture resembles fine bread crumbs. Tip into a bowl, stir in the toasted, chopped hazelnuts, and set aside.

Peel, core, and slice the apples, then scatter layers of apple and blackberries in a baking dish, sprinkling cinnamon between the layers.

Top with the crumble mixture in an even layer, then bake in the oven for about 50 minutes until the fruit is tender and bubbling and the crumble topping golden. Serve with thick cream or custard.

Sour cream apple cake

MAKES 1 x 8-INCH CAKE
⅓ cup (¾ stick) butter
2 tart cooking apples, peeled, cored, and sliced
6 tbsp. crème fraîche or sour cream
grated rind and juice of 1 lemon
¾ cup sugar
1½ tbsp. all-purpose flour
6 eggs, separated

FOR THE FILLING
1⅓ cups crème fraîche or sour cream
½ tsp. vanilla extract
4 tsp. sugar

FOR THE TOPPING
1 tbsp. sugar
1½ tsp. ground cinnamon
2 tbsp. slivered almonds

Heat the oven to 325°F. Grease and flour three 8-inch-diameter round cake pans with removable bottoms.

Melt the butter in a pan, add the apples, and cook gently for about 8 minutes, stirring, until pulpy. Beat together the crème fraîche, lemon rind and juice, sugar, flour, and egg yolks and stir into the apples. Heat gently, stirring, for about 5 minutes, until the mixture thickens. Set aside. Combine the topping ingredients in a bowl and set aside.

In a clean bowl, beat the egg whites until they form stiff peaks. Carefully fold them, a few tablespoons at a time, into the apple mixture. Divide among the prepared pans and spread out evenly. Scatter the prepared topping over one of the cakes, then bake all three in the oven for about 45 minutes, until firm and golden. Let cool in the pans, then carefully turn out of the pans. Cover with plastic wrap and leave in the fridge to chill.

Meanwhile, combine the filling ingredients in another clean bowl. Spread half on top of one of the plain cake layers, top with the second plain cake layer along with the remaining cream, and place the cinnamon-and-almond-topped cake layer on top. Slice and serve.

pears

Harvested in late summer and the fall, and available from cold-storage well into spring, pears are a boon during the colder months, when other fresh fruit is generally unavailable. These fragrant honeyed fruits come in a great variety of flavors, textures, and colors. Some have crisp white flesh, while others have a meltingly soft, almost grainy texture. They can be eaten raw or sliced and tossed into salads, and are particularly good combined with sharp-flavored cheeses. They are also delicious cooked—poached, pan-fried, in tarts and cakes, and with meat or game.

Pears should be picked and sold before they are fully ripe. When buying, look for firm fruits that you can take home to ripen. A pear will be yielding to the touch around the stem when ripe, but not soft. Really firm varieties, such as the bosc pear, are often the best for cooking.

Eaten raw, pears may be either peeled or eaten with their skins on. Many cooked recipes call for them to be peeled, which can be done simply with a vegetable peeler. The core is much smaller and tenderer than the apple core, and can be cut away easily if the fruit is quartered or cut into wedges. Halved pears can be cored using a melon baller, but to remove the core while leaving the pear whole—as may be required for poached pears—it is easiest to use a pointed apple corer or long vegetable peeler.

poached pears

Pears are delicious poached in a lightly spiced syrup and served hot or cold with cream or ice cream. This version uses white wine and fragrant star anise, but red wine and warm spices, such as cinnamon, work just as well. Peel 4 pears and remove the cores with an apple corer or long pointed vegetable peeler, leaving the fruits whole. Gently heat 2 cups of white wine and 2 tablespoons of granulated sugar in a pan, stirring, until the sugar has dissolved. Add the pears and 1 star anise and bring to a boil. Reduce the heat, cover, and simmer for 25-30 minutes, turning the pears once or twice, until tender. Lift out the pears and place in a dish. Increase the heat under the pan and boil the syrup for about 15 minutes until reduced and thickened. Pour it over the pears and serve hot or cold.

NOTES

Chocolate crêpes with caramelized pears

Pears and chocolate have a natural affinity. This is the perfect dessert to serve as a treat, when the nights are drawing in and the temperature is starting to drop.

SERVES 4
½ cup light cream
2 oz. dark chocolate (about ⅓ cup)
1 tbsp. corn syrup
1 tbsp. brandy
25g/1 oz. butter
4 pears, peeled, cored, and cut
into wedges

FOR THE CRÊPES
¾ cup all-purpose flour
pinch of salt
2 eggs, beaten
1¼ cups milk
butter, for frying

First make the crêpes. Sift the flour and salt into a bowl and make a well in the middle. Pour the beaten eggs and half the milk into the well and gradually mix in the flour to make a smooth batter. Whisk in the rest of the milk, then let stand for 20 minutes.

Heat a crêpe pan (or very small frying pan) until very hot, then add a little butter and wipe it over the surface with a piece of paper towel to leave a thin film. Add a small ladleful of batter to the pan, tipping the pan so that a thin even layer covers the bottom. Cook for about 1 minute, until golden underneath, then flip over and cook the other side for about 30 seconds, until golden. Slide onto a plate. Cook another seven crêpes in the same way, layering them between sheets of paper towel. Set aside and keep warm.

Put the cream, chocolate, syrup, and brandy in a pan and heat gently, stirring, until melted and combined. Set aside and keep warm.

Heat the butter in a frying pan, add the pears and fry on both sides until golden. Fold each crêpe into four to make a cone, fill with pears, drizzle with the chocolate sauce, and serve.

pear and blue cheese crostini

Ripe, juicy pears and blue cheese are great partners. Served together on little toasts, they make a superb accompaniment to pre-dinner drinks. Cut a small baguette into thick slices. Brush lightly with olive oil, then toast in the oven (or under a broiler) on both sides until golden. While still warm, top with a slither of Gorgonzola cheese and a small wedge of ripe pear. Serve immediately.

quinces

A frequently underrated autumn treat, the quince, a relative of the apple and pear, has a heady aroma and sharp citrusy flavor. It is said that quinces are at their best grown in cold climates so that they ripen very slowly, giving their intense fragrance and flavor time to develop. In unripe fruits, the yellow skin is covered with a downy coating, but this disappears as the fruit ripens, leaving a smooth skin like that of a pear.

Quinces are too tart to eat raw, so should always be cooked, usually with plenty of sugar. They are wonderful turned into a clear jelly and are the key ingredient in the coarse Spanish fruit "cheese" *membrillo*, which is traditionally served with slices of Manchego cheese as a tapas dish to accompany drinks. The Portuguese call the quince *marmelada*, revealing the heritage of the sticky orange marmalade that we know today, which was originally made with quinces. They are also wonderful cooked with poultry and game, and a quince sauce makes an excellent accompaniment to pork.

Quinces are more likely to found growing in private gardens than for sale on supermarket shelves, but they are well worth trying if you get the opportunity. Look for ripe yellow fruits. Be warned, though—as they tend to rot from the inside, even a fruit that looks blemish-free may be revealed as being no good when cut open.

To prepare, wash, then peel using a vegetable peeler. The fruit is surprisingly hard, so carefully cut into quarters using a sharp heavy knife and remove the core. Like that of apples and pears, the flesh browns when exposed to air. However, this is not a problem, as quince flesh turns a deep pinkish-amber when cooked and any previous dicoloration will go unnoticed.

baked quinces

This delicious dessert can be put together in a matter of minutes, then left to bake while the main course is eaten.

To prepare, beat together ⅓ cup (¾ stick) of butter, ¼ cup of brown sugar, and 2 teaspoons of ground cinnamon in a bowl until creamy. Cut 4 quinces in half, remove and discard the cores, and arrange in an ovenproof dish. Spread the cinnamon mixture on top and bake in a heated oven at 375°F for about 30 minutes, until tender. Serve.

NOTES

Roast duck breasts with quinces

Fragrant roast quinces are the perfect foil for the robust taste of tender juicy duck. The combination of honeyed quince and richly flavored duck in every mouthful is heavenly.

SERVES 4

4 duck breasts, about
7 oz. each
salt and freshly ground black pepper
1 tbsp. olive oil
3 quinces, peeled, cored,
and quartered
2 tsp. clear honey
juice of 1 lemon
1 tbsp. flour
2 tbsp. sherry
1 cup chicken stock

Heat the oven to 425°F.

Score the duck skin in a lattice pattern and season well with salt and pepper. Place the duck, skin-side up, in a roasting pan and spinkle the olive oil over it.

Place the quinces in a bowl. Combine the honey and half the lemon juice in a measuring cup, pour it over the quinces, and toss to coat. Nestle them around the duck and roast in the oven for about 20 minutes until the duck is cooked and the quinces tender.

Remove the duck and quinces to a serving dish, cover with foil, and keep warm. Make a gravy by pouring off all but 1–2 tablespoons of fat from the roasting pan, then place it over a low heat. Stir in the flour and cook for about 1 minute. Gradually stir in the sherry and stock and simmer for about 2 minutes until thickened. Remove from the heat, season to taste with salt and pepper and the remaining lemon juice, then serve with the duck and quinces.

membrillo

This thick quince jam is a specialty of Spain, traditionally served in slices with Manchego cheese. The sweetness of the *membrillo* is a perfect foil for the saltiness of the cheese. To make, line a rectangular dish or roasting pan with parchment paper. Put 2 pounds of peeled and chopped quinces in a large pan and cover with water. Bring to a boil, reduce the heat, and simmer until the fruit is soft. Drain well, then mash the fruit and press through a strainer to achieve a fine puree. Measure the puree and put into a clean pan with an equal volume of sugar. Heat gently, stirring continuously, until the puree turns a deep red color. Pour into the lined dish or pan to a depth of about 1 inch and let it cool.

autumn berries

Picking wild fruits from hedges and brambles is one of the best autumn activities. A pail of freshly gathered blackberries can be made into a fruity crumble, and hard bitter sloes can be dropped into gin to make a fragrant, ruby-red spirit, that is perfect for serving at Christmas. Rose hips, crab apples, and elderberries are all good for making into jelly.

The shiny globular blackberry—or bramble, as it is also known—is probably the most widely harvested and used of all fruits from hedges. It grows wild, but bushes are also cultivated. On their own, blackberries can have a slightly bland flavor, so they're frequently paired with other fruits such as apples. They do not keep well, and should be eaten within a day of picking or buying; discard any that are mushy. Blackberries do freeze well, however, and can be frozen in a single layer on a lined baking sheet, then transferred to a sealed bag or container and returned to the freezer for later use. As well as being good in fruit crumbles, blackberries are also delicious turned into preserves and cooked with other autumn berries, such as tiny black elderberries.

Rose hips are the fruits of the wild rose. They are mainly used for making a syrup, which can be diluted with water to make a fragrant drink, or used for flavoring milky desserts such as rice pudding or ice cream, or be made into jelly.

Tiny black sloes are a type of wild plum that grow widely in hedges throughout Europe. The raw fruit is mouth-puckeringly sour and bitter—but infused in gin, the flavor mellows, producing a delicious ruby-colored drink. Freezing is also said to mellow the flavor, so it may be worth freezing any picked before the first frosts for a couple of days before using.

sloe gin

To make sloe gin, wash and remove the stems from 1 pound of sloes (about 3 cups) and prick the fruits all over using a toothpick. Put in a large Mason jar or canning jar, sprinkle in 1 cup of sugar and add 1 liter of gin. Seal the jar and keep in a cool place. Shake every day for one week, then once a week for the next 2 months. At this stage, the liqueur is ready to drink but its flavor will improve with keeping, so, if you can, strain into bottles and let it mature for at least 6 months before drinking.

NOTES

Blackberry and elderberry jelly

MAKES ABOUT 2 LB.
2 lb. blackberries (about 7-8 cups)
8 oz. elderberries, stalks removed
(about 1-1½ cups)
seeds from 2 lemons
granulated sugar (see recipe)

Wash and pick over the fruit, discarding any over-ripe or mushy berries. Put into a large pan along with the lemon seeds. Pour in just enough water to cover, bring to a boil, then reduce the heat, cover, and let simmer gently for about 1 hour.

Remove from the heat, mash the fruit well with a potato masher, and let cool. Pour the mixture into a scalded jelly bag suspended over a large bowl and let it drain overnight.

Measure the strained juice from the bowl and pour it into a large pan. Add 2⅓ cups sugar for every 2½ cups juice, then heat gently, stirring, until the sugar has dissolved. Turn up the heat and let it boil rapidly until the temperature reaches 220°F (test with a candy thermometer). Remove from the heat, skim off any scum, and ladle the jelly into sterilized jars. Seal and let cool before labeling and storing in a cool dark place.

Rose hip syrup

MAKES ABOUT 10 CUPS
2 lb. rose hips (about 10 cups)
10 cups cold water
2⅓ cups granulated sugar

Wash and pick over the rose hips, discarding any that are brown and mushy. Put in a blender or food processor and blend until roughly chopped. Put in a pan, pour in 7 cups of the water and bring to a boil. Remove from the heat and let stand for 15 minutes, then pour into a jelly bag suspended over a large bowl and let it drain overnight.

Return the pulp in the jelly bag to the pan, pour in the remaining water, and bring to a boil. Let it stand for about 15 minutes, then drain through the jelly bag into the bowl.

Pour all the juice into a clean pan, add the sugar, and heat gently, stirring, until the sugar has dissolved. Bring to a boil and boil rapidly until the mixture has reduced to about 3½ cups. Pour the syrup into bottles, label, and store.

game

Game is traditionally associated with the colder months of the year and is in abundance during autumn and winter. Much game, such as rabbit, venison, quail, and duck, is now farmed, so is readily available outside the wild season, but some, such as jackrabbit and woodcock, is not and remains a seasonal treat. Wild game, however, is often considered to have by far the better flavor.

Game can be divided into two categories—furred and feathered. The furred variety includes boar, venison, rabbit, and jackrabbit, while the feathered includes all the game birds from pheasant, quail, and duck to woodcock, partridge, grouse, and pigeon.

Some people believe that to get the freshest and tastiest game they need to buy it still feathered or furred, and pluck, skin, and gut it themselves. However, for those that do not relish the idea of doing this, there are plenty of good butchers and game dealers where it can be bought ready-prepared. Most game should be hung for several days after killing in order to develop the flavor, but generally the butcher or game dealer will do this, too, both for game sold ready for cooking and for game that still needs preparing for the pot.

Venison sausages with sweet potato mash

SERVES 4
2 tbsp. olive oil
8-12 venison sausages
2 onions, cut in half and sliced
2 cloves garlic, sliced
1 tbsp. soft brown sugar
1 cup red wine
salt and freshly ground black pepper
3 sprigs of fresh thyme or ¼ tsp. dried thyme

FOR THE MASH
2¼ lb. sweet potatoes, peeled and cut into large chunks
salt
⅓ cup (¾ stick) butter
2 red chilies, seeded and finely chopped

Heat the oven to 375°F. Heat the oil in a large frying pan. Prick the sausages, add to the pan, and brown all over. Transfer to a baking dish and arrange in a single layer.

Toss the onions and garlic into the frying pan and cook gently, stirring occasionally, for about 10 minutes. Sprinkle in the sugar and cook, stirring, for another 5 minutes. Pour in the wine, season to taste with salt and pepper, if using the dried thyme add it now, and bring to a boil. Pour the mixture over the sausages, and if using the fresh thyme sprigs, tuck them in, then cover the dish with foil and bake in the oven for about 30 minutes.

About 15 minutes before the end of the cooking time, prepare the mash. Cook the sweet potatoes in boiling salted water for 10-15 minutes until tender, drain well, and mash. Melt the butter in a pan, add the chilies, and fry for 1-2 minutes, then stir into the potatoes. Serve with the sausages and onion gravy.

NOTES

Spiced braised duck with pears

SERVES 4

4 duck legs
salt and freshly ground black pepper
2 tbsp. olive oil
2 cloves garlic, crushed
1¾ cups chicken stock
1 tsp. ground ginger
2 tsp. ground cinnamon
½ tsp. smoked paprika
2 pears, cored, peeled, and quartered
1 tbsp. soft brown sugar

Heat the oven to 350°F. Season the duck legs with salt and pepper, then heat half the oil in a large frying pan. Add the duck and fry for about 5 minutes until well browned. Transfer to an ovenproof dish and arrange in a single layer. Drain most of the fat from the pan, add the garlic, and gently fry for 1 minute. Stir in the stock, ginger, cinnamon, and paprika, bring to a boil, then pour it over the duck. Bake in the oven for 1¼ hours.

About 10 minutes before the end of the cooking time, heat the remaining oil in a clean pan, add the pears, and fry for 5 minutes, until golden. Sprinkle in the sugar and cook for 4–5 minutes. Add the pears to the duck in the casserole dish and cook for 15 minutes, until the duck is cooked and the pears tender.

Lift out the duck and pears and transfer to a serving dish to keep warm. Skim the fat off the cooking juices, season with salt and pepper if needed, pour over the duck and pears, and serve.

North African-style pigeon pie

SERVES 6

3 pigeons, oven-ready
⅓ cup (¾ stick) butter
1 onion, chopped
1 cinnamon stick
½ tsp. ground ginger
1 tsp. paprika
1 tsp. ground coriander seed
handful of fresh flat-leaf parsley, chopped
6 eggs, beaten
salt and freshly ground black pepper
¾ cup almonds, toasted and roughly chopped
⅔ cup dried apricots, finely chopped
1 tsp. ground cinnamon, plus extra for dusting
12 sheets phyllo dough

Put the pigeons in a large pot with 2 tablespoons of the butter, the onion, spices (except for the ground cinnamon), and parsley. Add water to cover and bring to a boil. Reduce the heat, cover, and simmer for 1 hour. Transfer the birds to a board and strain and reserve the stock. Skin and bone the birds, chop the flesh into bite-size pieces, and set aside. Pour ⅔ cup of the stock into a clean pan and stir in the eggs. Heat gently, stirring, for about 25 minutes to form a thick sauce. Season well with salt and pepper. Heat the oven to 375°F.

Melt the remaining butter, and use it to brush the inside of a baking dish. Line the dish with 6 sheets of phyllo dough, brushing each sheet with butter and leaving any long pieces overhanging the dish. Spread half the pigeon meat over it, then sprinkle that with half the almonds, apricots, and cinnamon, and half the sauce. Top with the remaining pigeon, almonds, apricots, cinnamon, and sauce. Fold the overhanging dough over it, then top with the remaining dough, again brushing each sheet with butter. Bake in the oven for 45 minutes. Serve hot or warm, dusted with extra ground cinnamon.

Roast quail with sage and bacon (opposite)

SERVES 4
2 tbsp. olive oil
juice of 1 lemon
1 tsp. paprika
salt and freshly ground black pepper
8 quail, oven-ready
small bunch fresh sage
12 strips of bacon
1 tbsp. flour
½ cup red wine
1 cup chicken stock
1 tsp. soft brown sugar

Whisk together the oil, lemon juice, and paprika in a small bowl and season well with salt and pepper. Pour it over the quail, rubbing it inside and out, then let it marinate in the fridge for 30 minutes.

Heat the oven to 375°F. Put the quail in a roasting pan. Place 2-3 sage leaves on each bird, reserving some for garnishing. Lay the bacon strips on top and roast for 25 minutes in the oven. To test if the birds are cooked, pierce the thickest part of the thigh with a knife or skewer. The juices should run clear; if not, roast for another 5 minutes, then retest. Transfer to a serving plate and keep warm. Fry the reserved sage leaves in a little oil until crisp and set aside.

To make the gravy, place the roasting pan over a low heat if it's flameproof—if not, scrape the drippings into a frying pan. Stir in the flour and cook for 1 minute. Gradually stir in the wine and stock and cook, stirring, until the mixture thickens, then stir in the sugar and season with salt and pepper to taste. Pour into a gravy boat and serve with the quail, garnished with the fried sage leaves.

Rabbit stewed with tomatoes and garlic

SERVES 4
2-3 tbsp. olive oil
1½-lb. rabbit, cut up
1½ cups baby onions, peeled
3 cloves garlic, sliced
14-½ oz. can chopped tomatoes
¾ cup red wine
2 bay leaves
2-3 sprigs of fresh thyme
2 tsp. paprika
salt and freshly ground black pepper

Heat 2 tablespoons of the oil in a large pan or flameproof casserole dish. Add the pieces of rabbit and fry over medium heat until browned all over. Remove from the pan and set aside.

Reduce the heat, add the remaining oil if necessary, then add the onions and fry gently for 4-5 minutes until well browned. Add the garlic and fry for another 2 minutes, then add the tomatoes, red wine, bay leaves, sprigs of thyme, and paprika. Season well with salt and and pepper.

Return the rabbit to the pan, bring to a boil, then lower the heat, cover, and simmer gently for about 1 hour, until the rabbit is tender. Check the seasoning and serve.

NOTES

Winter

Winter is the time to stay in and enjoy warming substantial meals. The wonderful roots and tubers that now fill produce shelves make a hearty foundation for such feasts. The colder months are one of the best times to indulge in that tastiest and most versatile of tubers, the potato—boiled, mashed, or roasted. Parsnips, celeriac (celery root), salsifies, and Jerusalem artichokes, each with their own distinctive flavor, are wonderful, too, for providing substance and comfort, either on their own or mixed together. The other family of vegetables to take full advantage of in winter is the brassicas. These include green, white, and red cabbages, Asian greens, kale, Swiss chard, Brussels sprouts, and cauliflowers. Belgian endive and radicchio lend a juicy freshness to winter salads, while tender sweet leeks add an uplifting tang to numerous savory dishes, as well as making a satisfying accompaniment to rich meaty dishes. Also now at hand are bright-red cranberries and earthy chestnuts, for creating some of the most delicious desserts.

cabbages

Properly cooked, cabbages are one of the joys of winter. Although available for most of the year, with different varieties arriving in different seasons, it is in the cold winter months that cabbages really come into their own. Winter is also a time when one of the most glorious of all cabbages comes into season—dark-green crinkly-leafed savoy.

Part of the brassica family, along with kale, broccoli and Brussels sprouts, cabbages come in many shapes and forms, from the tightly packed, round heads of white cabbages to sweet pointed cabbages and dark purplish-red specimens with creamy-veined leaves.

Sometimes hearty and robust, sometimes sweet and delicate, cabbages make a good partner for roasted meats and warming stews and sit perfectly alongside roasted, boiled, or mashed root vegetables. It is a very versatile ingredient. Delicious served as an accompaniment, it also works well in soups, such as the Italian *ribollita* and Asian stir-fries. It can even be pickled and served as a relish, such as in German *sauerkraut* and Korean *kimchi*. Leftovers are often fried with cold potatoes to make the classic bubble and squeak or can be combined with mashed potatoes and sautéed onions, then shaped into a patty and fried to make the Irish dish colcannon.

Stuffed cabbage leaves (opposite)

SERVES 4

1 savoy or other green cabbage
14 oz. good-quality pork sausages
3 shallots, finely chopped
¼ cup bread crumbs
pinch of freshly grated nutmeg
2 tbsp. grated Parmesan cheese
salt and freshly ground black pepper
pinch of dried thyme, or the leaves from a few sprigs of fresh thyme
14½-oz. can chopped tomatoes
⅓ cup white wine

Cut away the core from the cabbage and carefully peel away the leaves, keeping them whole. Blanch the leaves by plunging them into boiling water for about 2 minutes, until just tender. Drain well and set aside.

Squeeze the sausage meat from the skins and combine with the shallots, bread crumbs, nutmeg, and Parmesan cheese in a bowl. Season with black pepper, then shape the mixture into eight egg-shaped balls.

Wrap each ball in 1 or 2 cabbage leaves and arrange in the bottom of a large pan. Sprinkle in the thyme, then pour in the tomatoes and wine and season with salt and pepper to taste. Cover and simmer for about 1 hour. Serve hot.

Thai-style duck curry with cabbage

SERVES 4

5 cups chicken stock
1 tbsp. sweet chili sauce
3 kaffir lime leaves, shredded
2 red chilies, seeded and
finely chopped
1 lemongrass stalk, finely chopped
1 shallot, finely chopped
1 clove garlic, finely chopped
2 duck breasts, about 7 oz. each
salt
2 tbsp. Thai fish sauce
1 tsp. soft brown sugar
juice of ½-1 lime
6 oz. savoy or pointed cabbage,
shredded (about 2¾-3 cups)
3 carrots, sliced diagonally
8 oz. cauliflower or broccoli, cut
into bite-size florets
(about 3-4 cups)
rice, for serving

Put the chicken stock, chili sauce, lime leaves, chilies, lemongrass, shallot, and garlic in a pan, bring to a boil, then reduce the heat and let simmer for about 20 minutes.

Meanwhile, score the skin of the duck breasts and rub with salt. Heat a large frying pan and add the duck, skin-side down. Cook for 10 minutes, then turn over and cook for another 3-4 minutes. Remove to a board, let cool slightly, and cut into bite-size pieces.

Strain the stock into a clean pan, then stir in the fish sauce, sugar, and lime juice to taste. Add the shredded cabbage, carrots, cauliflower or broccoli florets, and the chopped duck. Cover and simmer for about 3 minutes, until the vegetables are tender but still crisp. Serve immediately with rice.

coleslaw

A classic crunchy coleslaw makes a perfect, refreshing salad. To prepare, shred ½ green cabbage and combine with 3 grated carrots, 1 thinly sliced red onion, and a handful of golden raisins. In a separate bowl, combine ⅔ cup of mayonnaise with the grated rind and juice of ½ lemon. Stir this mixture into the vegetables to combine well, chill, and serve.

NOTES

cabbage braised with wine and pancetta

This is one of the simplest and most delicious methods of cooking cabbages, and savoy or pointed cabbages are particularly good served in this way. Brussels sprouts and kale may be given the same treatment, too. For a vegetarian version, shredded sun-dried tomatoes can be substituted for the pancetta. Simply fry a few handfuls of chopped pancetta in 2 tablespoons of olive oil for 2 minutes, then add 3 finely chopped shallots, and cook for another 3-4 minutes. Shred a medium-sized cabbage and toss into the pan, then cook, stirring, for about 3 minutes. Add 1 cup of white wine, season with salt and pepper to taste, cover, and cook for about 10 minutes until the cabbage is sweet, juicy, and tender, but not soft. Serve immediately.

Sweet-and-sour red cabbage

Red cabbage cooked with apple is a delicious vibrant accompaniment to roast meats. The rich lively flavors make it particularly well suited to fattier meats such as goose, duck, and pork, although it is also great with leaner poultry such as chicken and turkey, and it is wonderful served cold with wafer-thin slices of cooked ham. Unlike most green cabbages, which generally suit fairly brief cooking, red cabbages are quite tough, so should be stewed slowly and gently for a long period of time.

SERVES 4

2 tbsp. olive oil
1 onion, chopped
2 cloves garlic, finely chopped
1 cooking apple, peeled and chopped
½ large red cabbage, thinly sliced
1 cup red wine
½ tbsp. soft brown sugar
2 tbsp. red wine vinegar
2 whole cloves
5 juniper berries, crushed
2-3 tbsp. golden raisins
salt and freshly ground black pepper

Heat the oil in a large pot. Add the onion and garlic and cook gently for about 5 minutes until soft. Toss in the apple, cabbage, wine, sugar, vinegar, cloves, juniper berries, and raisins. Season to taste with salt and pepper and stir to combine.

Bring to a gentle simmer, cover, and let cook for about 40-45 minutes, stirring once or twice during the cooking time, until the cabbage is really tender and sweet. If necessary, add a splash more water towards the end of the cooking time to prevent the cabbage sticking to the bottom of the pot. Check the seasoning, add extra salt and pepper if needed, and serve hot or cold.

kale

Another member of the cabbage family, hardy kale thrives in the depths of winter when little else will grow, and is available from late autumn right through until early spring. Its flavor, in fact, improves after a good frost, making it perfect as a cold-weather treat. There are several varieties, including the widely available dark-green curly kale with its sprawling stems and the less common blue-green "black" kale, better known as *cavalo nero*. Like cabbage, it is good served as an accompaniment, but is also delicious added to soups, such as the classic Italian *ribollita*, and the similar Portuguese *caldo verde*.

To prepare kale, strip out the tough, stringy central stalks and keep only the dark-green leaves. Shred coarsely and cook in boiling salted water for about 4 minutes, until just tender. Drain well, then melt some butter in a pan, toss in the cooked kale, and cook for another 1–2 minutes to heat through. Season with plenty of black pepper and serve immediately.

Portuguese kale soup *(opposite)*

Based on the classic Portuguese soup *caldo verde*, this hearty soup is a fabulous way to use up the green curly kale that proliferates on produce shelves during the cold winter months. Other cabbages, such as savoy or *cavalo nero*, will do just as well in this recipe, so substitute it if available. Or, if an Italian-style *ribollita* is preferred, just add a can of chopped tomatoes with the stock, and use a can of drained cannellini beans in place of the potatoes. Blend half the beans to thicken the soup, and leave the rest whole.

SERVES 4
1¼ lb. floury potatoes
2 tbsp. olive oil
4 cloves garlic, finely chopped
1 onion, finely chopped
4¾ cups vegetable stock
8 oz. kale, shredded
(about 3–4 cups)
salt and freshly ground black pepper
8 thin slices chorizo, cut
into strips

Peel and chop the potatoes, then set on one side. Heat the oil in a large pot. Add the garlic and onion and gently fry for about 5 minutes, until soft. Add the potatoes and stock and let simmer gently for about 20 minutes, until the potatoes are tender.

Transfer to a food processor or blender and blend until smooth. Return to the pot. Stir in the kale and cook for about 10 minutes until the kale is tender, but not soft. Season to taste with salt and pepper, then ladle the soup into warm serving bowls, Scatter in the chorizo and serve.

NOTES

brussels sprouts

Growing up a thick central stalk, Brussels sprouts are in fact tiny cabbages with tightly packed leaves. They help brighten up the chilly months, providing an elegant alternative to their larger relations, and are a traditional favorite on the winter festive table. Like all members of the cabbage family, they can reveal sulphurous undertones if overcooked but, when cooked to perfection, they are truly sweet and tender. The green leaves shooting from the top of the stalks —in England known as sprout tops—can also be eaten, traditionally at the end of winter when all the sprouts themselves have been picked off.

When buying, look for small, firm specimens with fresh-looking leaves and avoid any that are yellowing. To prepare, remove the sprouts from the stalks and peel away any tough outer leaves to reveal the crisp, tightly packed heads. Some people cut a cross into the bottom to help heat to penetrate and speed up cooking, but this is really unnecessary. To cook whole, boil in salted water for about 5 minutes until just tender, then toss with butter and toasted slivered almonds or hazelnuts, if you like. Bear in mind that sprouts will continue to cook in their residual heat after draining, so be careful not to overdo them. As well as boiled, sprouts can be stir-fried, or cooked then mixed into a creamy sauce for a gratin, or made into soup. Sprout tops are best lightly steamed and served tossed in a little butter with a sprinkling of black pepper.

Fragrant stir-fried sprouts

SERVES 4
2 tbsp. vegetable oil
2 strips of bacon, cut up into small pieces
2 cloves garlic, sliced
1 tsp. coriander seeds, lightly crushed
1 lb. Brussels sprouts, shredded (about 3-4 cups)
salt and freshly ground black pepper

Heat the oil in a wok, then add the bacon pieces and fry for about 2 minutes until golden. Add the garlic and coriander seeds and toss over the heat for a further 30 seconds or so.

Add the shredded sprouts and stir-fry for 1-2 minutes, until they are just tender. Season to taste with salt and pepper and serve immediately.

cauliflowers

Available almost all year round, with different varieties arriving in each season, the creamy-white cauliflower with its encircling band of thick green leaves is another member of the cabbage family that is a staple of the colder months. Like broccoli, the tightly packed cauliflower head consists of unopened flower buds.

Delicious eaten raw or lightly cooked in salads, or served as crudités and used for scooping up creamy dips, cauliflowers are amazingly versatile. Originating in Arabia, it suits both European-style cooking and the spices of the East. In Indonesia, it is blanched, added to the classic salad *gado gado,* and served with spicy peanut dressing. In the Middle East, it may be pickled with salt, vinegar, and chilies, or deep-fried as fritters. The cooked florets are often paired with a creamy or cheesy sauce or may be sprinkled with chopped hard-boiled eggs or garlicky bread crumbs.

Winter varieties of cauliflowers usually have a more pronounced flavor than those grown in other seasons. When buying, look out for crisp young heads, surrounded by fresh-looking green leaves, and avoid those with dark spots. To prepare, trim away the tough outer leaves and leave small heads whole or break larger ones into florets. Either steam or blanch in boiling salted water for a few minutes until sweet and tender, but still retaining some bite. Be careful not to overcook.

cauliflower in cheese sauce

To make a simple cheesy cauliflower gratin, just cut a large head of a cauliflower into florets and boil in salted water for about 5 minutes until tender. Then drain well and toss with about ¼ cup of crème fraîche or sour cream and about ½ cup of grated Gruyère (or Swiss) cheese. Season to taste with salt and freshly ground black pepper and turn into an ovenproof dish. Sprinkle another ½ cup of grated Gruyère over it, grind a little more black pepper over it, and bake in a heated oven at 400°F for about 15 minutes until golden and bubbling.

NOTES

mustard pickle (chow chow)

There are numerous cauliflower pickles, from Middle Eastern _torshi_, a spicy ruby-stained mix of cabbages and cauliflowers colored from beets, to this bright-yellow sweet and fragrant mustard pickle packed with crispy chopped vegetables.

MAKES ABOUT 4 LB.
8 oz. salt (¾–1 cup)
1 cauliflower, cut into small florets
12 oz. pearl onions (about 3 cups), peeled
4 oz. chopped gherkins (about 1 cup)
2 lb. mixed vegetables, such as cucumbers, green beans, zucchinis, green bell peppers, and celeriac, prepared and chopped
3 cups cider vinegar
¾ cup sugar
2 tsp. mustard powder
1 tsp. coriander seed, crushed
1 tsp. ground ginger
2 cloves garlic, finely chopped
3 tbsp. all-purpose flour
½ tbsp. turmeric

Put the salt and 2½ quarts of water in a large bowl or pot and stir until the salt has dissolved. Add the cauliflower, onions, gherkins, and mixed vegetables, stir, then weigh it down with a plate and leave it soaking for 24 hours. Drain, rinse thoroughly in cold water, and drain again.

Put the vinegar, sugar, mustard powder, coriander seed, ginger, and garlic in a large pot and heat gently, stirring, until the sugar has dissolved. Add the drained vegetables, bring to a boil, then reduce the heat and simmer gently for about 7 minutes.

Mix the flour and turmeric with about ¼ cup cold water in a small bowl, then stir this mixture into the pot of vegetables and let it simmer for another 5 minutes, until thick.

Spoon the mixture into warmed sterilized jars, cover, seal, and label. Store in a cool dark place for at least 2 weeks before serving. Once a jar is opened, store in the refrigerator.

cauliflower pakoras

In India, cauliflower florets, coated in a spiced batter and deep-fried, make a popular snack. To prepare, put 1¼ cups of garbanzo bean flour in a bowl with 3 tablespoons of all-purpose flour, 2 teaspoons of ground cumin, and a pinch of turmeric, and stir to combine. Gradually whisk in 1½ cups of cold water to make a smooth batter. Dip the cauliflower florets in the batter and deep-fry in hot oil for about 5 minutes until puffed up and golden. Serve with mango chutney or _raita_.

leeks

Long creamy leeks with their mild oniony flavor make their first appearance in the closing days of autumn and last through winter into the spring. They may be sold still muddy from the earth with their green outer leaves still attached, or washed and neatly trimmed, and they range in size from tiny delicate sticks, about the size of a large scallion, to long fat giants. Chopped, they can be used like onions to add a refreshing tang to any dish, such as an omelet, savory tart, gratin, or soup. Cooked whole, then wrapped in ham and baked in a creamy sauce, they are transformed into a superb supper dish. But they are also delicious served on their own as a vegetable accompaniment, sautéed or even braised in a splash of wine.

Most recipes call only for the pale, tightly furled part of the leek, while the tough, green outer leaves are usually discarded. Even leeks sold cleaned up are likely to have some soil still trapped between their closely wrapped layers, so always wash them well before using. Starting at the top, slit down the leek lengthwise, then wash under cold running water, flushing out all traces of dirt. If a recipe calls for sliced leeks, cut them up first, then rinse away any soil.

Leek and sun-dried tomato frittata (opposite)

SERVES 4
2 tbsp. olive oil
3 leeks, thinly sliced
6 sun-dried (sun-blushed) tomatoes in olive oil, drained and shredded
handful of fresh flat-leaf parsley, roughly chopped, plus extra for garnishing
salt and freshly ground black pepper
6 eggs, beaten

Heat the olive oil in a 9-inch-diameter frying pan. Add the leeks and cook gently for about 10 minutes until tender. Stir in the sun-dried tomatoes and parsley and season well with salt and pepper.

Heat the broiler to hot. Pour the eggs over the vegetables in the frying pan, stirring slightly to combine. Cook gently for about 10 minutes, pushing the edges into the middle as they set and letting the uncooked egg run underneath, until the bottom is firm but the frittata is still moist on top.

Place the frittata under the broiler and cook for about 5 minutes until set and golden on top. Carefully turn out of the pan onto a plate, then flip over onto another plate so it sits rightside-up. Garnish with parsley, cut into wedges, and serve.

NOTES

Glamorgan sausages

2 tbsp. sunflower oil, plus extra for
frying
2 leeks, finely chopped
1⅓ cups bread crumbs, plus extra for
coating
6 oz. Caerphilly cheese, crumbled
(about 1⅔ cups)
½ tsp. dried oregano
salt and freshly ground black pepper
2 eggs, beaten

FOR THE SAUCE
2 tbsp. olive oil
½ onion, finely chopped
14½-oz. can chopped tomatoes
3 tbsp. vermouth
pinch of sugar
½ tsp. dried oregano

Heat 1 tablespoon of the oil in a pan. Add the leeks and cook gently for about 7 minutes, until tender. Tip into a bowl and combine with the bread crumbs, cheese, and oregano, seasoning to taste with salt and pepper. Gradually add some of the beaten eggs, until the mixture comes together but is not too wet.

Shape the mixture into 8 sausages, then dip them in the remaining beaten egg and roll in bread crumbs to coat. Leave in the fridge to chill for at least 30 minutes.

Meanwhile make the sauce. Heat the oil in a pan, add the onion and fry for about 5 minutes, until soft. Toss in the tomatoes, vermouth, sugar, and oregano, then season to taste with salt and pepper and let it simmer gently for about 20 minutes. Set aside and keep warm.

Heat a little sunflower oil in a large frying pan. Add the chilled sausages and cook for about 5-7 minutes, until crisp and golden all over. Serve immediately with the sauce.

Vichyssoise

Leeks seem to have been created for turning into soups—and there are countless recipes. This French classic is traditionally served chilled, but can be heated up on colder days.

SERVES 4
¼ cup (½ stick) butter
1 onion, chopped
3 large leeks, sliced
1 potato, cut into chunks
3 cups vegetable stock
1¼ cups milk
about ½ cup light cream
juice of ½ lemon
salt and freshly ground black pepper
small handful of fresh chives,
chopped, for garnishing

Melt the butter in a large pot. Add the onion and leeks, then fry gently for about 5 minutes, until tender. Add the potato and stock, cover, and let it simmer for about 15 minutes, until the potato is tender.

Tip the contents of the pot into a blender or food processor and blend until smooth. Transfer to a large bowl, stir in the milk, cream, and lemon juice, and season to taste with salt and pepper. Let it chill in the fridge for at least 2 hours.

The soup will have thickened from standing, so add a splash more milk if needed. Check the seasoning and add extra salt, pepper, and lemon juice, if needed. Serve sprinkled with the chives.

NOTES

Trout baked in paper with leeks and carrots

SERVES 4
2 tbsp. sunflower oil
2 large leeks, finely sliced
1-inch piece fresh ginger, peeled and finely grated
3 carrots, cut into fine matchsticks
1 tsp. sesame oil
salt and freshly ground black pepper
4 trout fillets, about 6 oz. each, skinned
juice of 1½ limes

Heat the oven to 400°F and cut out four 14-inch squares of parchment paper or foil.

Heat the oil in a pan, add the leeks and ginger, and fry gently for about 10 minutes, until soft. Stir in the carrots and sesame oil, season to taste with salt and pepper, and remove from the heat. Divide the vegetables among the sheets of parchment paper, making a pile in the center of each sheet.

Lay a fillet of fish on top of each pile of vegetables, season with salt and pepper, and sprinkle with lime juice. Fold the paper over the fish, twisting the edges together to make a tightly sealed package. Place on a baking sheet and bake in the oven for about 15 minutes, until the fish is cooked through. Put each wrapped fillet on a warm plate and serve immediately.

Cock-a-leekie

This traditional Scottish soup, which comes somewhere between a chunky broth and a wholesome stew, makes the most of some of winter's finest ingredients, combining barley, chicken, tender leeks, and sweet juicy prunes.

SERVES 4
½ cup barley
5 cups chicken stock
1 bay leaf
1 tsp. dried thyme
4 juniper berries, crushed
3 large leeks, sliced
¾ cup ready-to-eat prunes, cut into bite-size pieces
14 oz. cooked chicken, cut into bite-size pieces (about 2½-3 cups)
freshly ground black pepper

Put the barley, stock, bay leaf, thyme, and juniper berries in a large pot, bring to a boil, then reduce the heat, cover, and let simmer for about 25 minutes, until the barley is tender.

Add the leeks, prunes, and chicken, recover the pot, and let it simmer for about 10 minutes, until the leeks are tender. Season with plenty of black pepper, ladle into bowls, and serve.

swiss chard

A member of the beet family, lush leafy Swiss chard is available from late autumn through into spring. With its thick, juicy, white stems and dark-green leaves, it offers a lighter alternative to other winter greens. You can also find red chard, with pinky-red stalks and veins, but despite its stunning appearance, its flavor is less good than that of the white-stalked green variety.

Chard leaves have a similar taste to spinach, although they are more robust in texture, and the juicy stalks are tender and mild, not unlike asparagus. Look for mature leaves with thick, lush stems. Smaller specimens with thinner stalks are good, too, but the juicy stems are one of the main delights of chard. Leaves should be shiny; avoid any with dark or slimy spots.

Cut off and discard the tough tips of the stems, wash the chard thoroughly, and drain well, shaking off as much water as possible, before cooking. Young tender chard leaves can be cooked whole, but with older ones, the tougher stem should be cut off, sliced, and tossed into the pan for a minute or so before the softer green part of the leaf. Chard, like spinach, reduces significantly with cooking, so allow what may seem to be an over-generous quantity per person.

Swiss chard with tomatoes, garbanzo beans, and spicy sausage

SERVES 4

1¼ lb. spicy pork sausages
2 tbsp. olive oil
1 onion, chopped
3 cloves garlic, chopped
14½-oz. can chopped tomatoes
15-oz. can garbanzo beans, drained and rinsed
18 oz. Swiss chard, sliced
crusty bread, for serving

Heat the broiler until hot and cook the sausages for about 10–15 minutes until well browned all over. Slice into ½-inch-thick chunks and set aside.

Heat the oil in a large pan. Add the onion and garlic and fry gently for about 5 minutes, until soft. Add the tomatoes, garbanzo beans, and sausages, and let simmer for about 10 minutes. Toss in the Swiss chard and cook for another 10 minutes, stirring occasionally, until the leaves are tender. Serve piping hot with crusty bread.

NOTES

belgian endive and radicchio

These two crisp salad vegetables are related and, despite their differences in appearance, share a distinctive bitter flavor. Plump, bullet-shaped Belgian endive (called chicory in England), with its tightly packed, green- or yellow-tinged white leaves, is used in both salads and cooked dishes. Belgian endive was originally grown just for its bitter roots, which were ground and added to coffee. Belgian endive is the shoot of the plant, first cultivated in Belgium and grown in darkness to achieve its pale color and more mellow flavor.

Vibrant red radicchio, with its white-veined leaves, may also be used in salads or cooked, although it has a more bitter flavor than Belgian endive.

Although Belgian endive and radicchio are available all year, they are particularly valuable in the winter, when so few other fresh salad greens are available. The long pointed leaves of Belgian endive are also excellent served as part of a selection of crudités for scooping up creamy dips. The whole heads are excellent cooked, too, either braised, roasted, or baked in a gratin.

Choose only firm white Belgian endive, avoiding any that are beginning to wilt or turn brown. Radicchio should be a rich red, also without any brown patches. To prepare, slice off the root end, rinse, and pat dry with paper towels, then use according to the recipe or divide into leaves for a salad.

roast buttered belgian endive

Allow 1 large or 2 small heads of Belgian endive per person. Cut large heads into quarters and small ones in half, then arrange in a baking dish and cover with thin shavings of butter. Season well with salt and pepper, cover, then bake in a heated oven at 375°F until tender and golden. This simple method of preparation can also be used to turn radicchio into something extra-special.

NOTES

Belgian endive salad with pear and walnut

It is easy to miss the refreshing taste of crunchy salads and sweet juicy fruits during the colder months of the year, so this crisp zesty salad provides a really special treat. Served as an appetizer or accompaniment, it offers a delicious contrast to winter's hearty root vegetables, brassicas, and stews.

SERVES 4

4 small handfuls of watercress
4 heads of Belgian endive
2 pears
½ cup walnut pieces
½ cup shaved Parmesan or Romano cheese

FOR THE DRESSING

1½ tbsp. lemon juice
½ tsp. honey
¼ cup olive oil
salt and freshly ground black pepper

First make the dressing by whisking together the lemon juice, honey, and olive oil in small bowl. Season to taste with salt and pepper and set aside.

Put a handful of watercress on each serving plate. Divide the Belgian endive into leaves and arrange on top. Peel and core the pears, then slice into slim wedges and scatter these over the leaves.

Scatter the walnuts and cheese shavings on top, then drizzle with the dressing and serve.

Creamy baked Belgian endive

You can use either Belgian endive or radicchio in this recipe. Baked with crème fraîche and Parmesan cheese, either vegetable makes a great partner to robust meat and game dishes.

SERVES 4

4 large heads of Belgian endive or radicchio
½ cup crème fraîche or sour cream
1 cup grated Parmesan cheese
freshly ground black pepper

Heat the oven to 400°F. Cut the Belgian endive or radicchio heads in half lengthwise and plunge into a pan of boiling salted water for about 2 minutes. Drain well and pat dry with paper towels.

Arrange in a baking dish, spoon the crème fraîche over the top, sprinkle with the Parmesan, and pepper it to taste, then bake in the oven for about 15 minutes, until the Belgian endive or radicchio is tender and the dish is crisp and well browned on top. Serve.

asian greens

A whole array of Asian greens is widely available right through the winter months. They are fabulous cooked lightly in Asian-style broths and stir-fries, or simple served on their own as a vegetable accompaniment. Many are related to the cabbage family.

Bok choy, choy sum, and Chinese broccoli (also known as Chinese kale) all have dark-green leaves and a mild flavor and are good stir-fried, added to soups, or blanched, as well as served alone, perhaps drizzled with a little sesame oil and a sprinkling of chili. Chinese mustard greens (also known as bamboo mustard and leaf mustard) have a more fiery flavor, with a distinct mustardy punch. Young leaves may be added to salads, while older leaves are better stir-fried. The pale-green Chinese cabbage (also known as napa cabbage) grows in large heads, rather like an elongated lettuce with a thick central rib. The leaves are tender, while the white rib is crisp. The vegetable has a faintly cabbage-like flavor and is good sliced and added to salads or stir-fried for a few minutes until just tender but retaining some bite.

When choosing any Asian greens, look for fresh-looking specimens with lush green leaves. Avoid any that are wilting, yellowing, or have soft slimy patches. Depending on size, bok choy can be cooked whole, cut in half, divided into separate leaves, or sliced. Its thick stems require slightly longer cooking than the dark-green leaves, so these are usually added to the pan a few minutes before the rest. Choy sum should be trimmed of its stalks and the leaves shredded before cooking. Chinese broccoli can be divided into florets, stems, and leaves (which should be shredded), all of which can be cooked separately. To prepare Chinese or napa cabbage, simply slice as thickly as required across the head.

bok choy with coconut dressing

This delicious vegetable accompaniment is very quick to prepare. Just combine ¼ cup of coconut milk with the juice of ½ lime and 1 teaspoon of Oriental fish sauce. If you like, add ½ chopped, seeded red chili as well. Divide the bok choy into leaves, then plunge into boiling water for 30–60 seconds until the leaves are just starting to wilt. Drain well, then drizzle with the coconut dressing. Toss to combine and serve immediately.

NOTES

Stir-fried bok choy with garlic and gingered beef

Also known as _pak choi_, _bok choy_ is probably one of the most widely available Asian greens. You can, however, substitute others in this recipe. If a more fiery result is preferred, try using Chinese mustard greens (bamboo mustard), or for a milder, sweeter flavor, use Chinese (or napa) cabbage leaves instead of the _bok choy_.

SERVES 4

2 cloves garlic, crushed
1-inch piece fresh ginger, peeled and grated
2 red chilies, seeded and finely chopped
1 tbsp. Oriental fish sauce
1 tsp. sesame oil
1 tbsp. soft brown sugar
3 tbsp. sunflower oil
1 lb. tenderloin steak
4 large heads of _bok choy_
steamed rice or noodles, for serving

Prepare a marinade by combining the garlic, ginger, chilies, fish sauce, sesame oil, sugar, and 1 tablespoon of the sunflower oil in a small bowl. Set aside.

Place the steak between two sheets of plastic wrap and beat with a mallet or rolling pin until thin. Cut into thin strips. Add to the marinade, toss to combine, and leave in the fridge to marinate for at least 1 hour.

Divide the _bok choy_ into leaves. Cut off the white fleshy part and slice it diagonally. Also slice up the larger leaves. Set aside.

Heat 1 tablespoon of the remaining oil in a wok. Add the beef along with the marinade and stir-fry for 2–3 minutes until medium-rare, then remove to a warmed plate. If necessary, add a little more oil to the wok, then add the white part of the _bok choy_ and stir-fry for about 1 minute. Add the green part of the leaves and stir-fry for another 30 seconds, or until the leaves start to wilt. Toss in the beef, check the seasoning, then serve with rice or noodles.

potatoes

Potatoes have been a staple in Europe since they were imported in the 16th century from South America, where they had been cultivated for several thousand years. Their popularity spread rapidly and, as a result, there are countless classic dishes in which they are the central ingredient, ranging from Irish champ and Scottish stovies to the French *pommes dauphinoises*. They are also delicious simply boiled or steamed and served with a pat of butter and a sprinkling of fresh herbs, or mashed with butter and milk. Parboiled and roasted in oil, they become wonderfully crisp and golden on the outside, while remaining floury and light inside. Thinly sliced and baked with onions and cream, they make a perfect partner to roasted meats, or try baking them whole, then stuffing them with all sorts of savory fillings. Sometimes they are added to soups and stews as a thickener, and are even used in pudding and cakes.

Always choose firm specimens with few blemishes and store in a cool, dark place until ready to use. The peeled flesh of potatoes discolors when exposed to air, so either peel and prepare just before using, or peel and leave in a large bowl of cold water until ready to cook.

rösti potatoes

These elegant little potato cakes, very similar to latkes, are a great accompaniment and also make a stunning appetizer when topped with a spoonful of sour cream, a slither of smoked salmon, and a sprinkling of chopped chives and lemon juice. To prepare, grate 1 pound of floury potatoes and ½ onion into a large bowl. Mix to combine, season well with salt, and leave for about 20 minutes. Squeeze hard to extract as much liquid as possible, then mix in 1 egg, 2 tablespoons of flour, and some freshly ground black pepper.

Heat about an inch of oil in a large frying pan. Add several tablespoons of the potato mixture, shaping them into cakes with the back of the spoon, and fry for 1–2 minutes on each side, until crisp and golden. Drain on paper towels and keep warm while you cook the remaining mixture in the same way. Serve immediately.

NOTES

Roast beef with garlic potatoes

SERVES 4-6

2³⁄₄ lb. potatoes, sliced (about
⅛-inch thick)
2 tbsp. butter
4 cloves garlic, thinly sliced
2 tsp. fresh thyme leaves
salt and freshly ground black
pepper
1¾ cups hot beef stock
2 lb. beef rump

Heat the oven to 375°F and grease a large baking dish. Arrange a layer of potatoes in the bottom of the dish, dot with a little butter, and scatter in some garlic and thyme. Repeat with layers of potato, butter, garlic, and thyme until they are all used up, seasoning as you go with salt and pepper. Pour in the stock. Cover with foil and cook in the oven for about 40 minutes.

Increase the oven temperature to 400°F and cook for another 15 minutes. Meanwhile, season the beef with ground black pepper.

Remove the dish from the oven, uncover it, and lay the beef on top of the potatoes. Return to the oven and roast for 20 minutes, then reduce the heat to 375°F and cook for another 20 minutes.

Remove the beef to a board and let it rest for about 10 minutes before carving, leaving the potatoes in the oven to keep warm while the meat rests. Serve.

Potato and cauliflower curry

SERVES 4

2 tbsp. sunflower oil
½ tsp. dried red pepper flakes
2 cloves garlic, finely chopped
2 tsp. grated fresh ginger
1 lb. potatoes, cut into ³⁄₄-inch cubes
½ cup water
2 tsp. ground cumin
1 tsp. ground coriander seed
½ tsp. turmeric
¼ tsp. salt
1 cauliflower, broken into florets
½ lemon
handful of fresh cilantro, chopped
rice or Indian breads, for serving

Heat the oil in a large pot and fry the red pepper flakes for about 10 seconds. Add the garlic and ginger, stir-fry for another 20 seconds or so, and stir in the potatoes.

Pour in the water and stir in the cumin, ground coriander seed, turmeric, and salt. Stir in the cauliflower and bring to a boil. Reduce the heat, cover, and simmer gently, stirring occasionally, for about 20 minutes until the vegetables are tender.

Squeeze in lemon juice to taste, sprinkle with fresh cilantro and serve with rice or Indian breads.

celeriac (celery root)

Knobbly celeriac, with its thick brown skin, may lack visual appeal, but under that outer coating is a mild creamy-white vegetable with a subtle celery-like flavor, that is sweet and crisp when eaten raw and meltingly soft and smooth when cooked. It is delicious made into a puree with butter, cream, and seasoning, or roasted with other roots until crisp and golden.

Buy celeriac with the smoothest skin available, so there is less waste when peeling. The skin is thicker than that of other root vegetables and is better peeled off using a sharp knife rather than a vegetable peeler. Cut into quarters first so that the thickness of the skin is clearly visible, then cut it away. Once exposed to air, the creamy flesh discolors rapidly, so put the prepared celeriac right into a bowl of water to which a little lemon juice has been added.

Fish pie topped with creamy celeriac mash *(opposite)*

SERVES 4

2 tbsp. olive oil
1 onion, chopped
2 cloves garlic, chopped
2 x 14½-oz. cans chopped tomatoes
½ tsp. ground cinnamon
¼ tsp. turmeric
¼ tsp. ground ginger
salt and freshly ground black pepper
11 oz. celeriac chopped (about 2½–3 cups)
11 oz. carrots, chopped (about 2–2½ cups)
1 lb. potatoes, chopped
2 tbsp. butter
2 tbsp. crème fraîche or sour cream
18 oz. firm white fish, such as haddock or hoki, skinned
9 oz. cooked, peeled jumbo shrimp (about 2 cups)

Heat the oven to 400°F. Heat the oil in a large pan, add the onion and garlic, and fry gently for 5 minutes, until soft. Add the tomatoes, cinnamon, turmeric, and ginger and season to taste with salt and pepper. Bring to a boil, then reduce the heat and simmer for about 20 minutes until thick. Set aside.

Meanwhile, put the celeriac, carrots, and potatoes in a pan, add ¼ cup water, cover tightly, and cook, shaking the pan frequently, for about 20 minutes, until the vegetables are tender. Check towards the end of the cooking time and add more water if necessary to prevent the vegetables from burning. Add the butter and mash well, then stir in the crème fraîche and season to taste with salt and pepper.

Put the fish into a clean pan, add enough water just to cover, bring to a gentle simmer, and cook for 3–4 minutes, then drain well and flake into large chunks. Gently fold the fish with the shrimp into the tomato sauce and transfer to a baking dish.

Spread the celeriac mash over the fish and bake in the oven for about 30 minutes until crisp and golden on top. Serve.

NOTES

jerusalem artichokes

Unrelated to the globe artichoke (see page 38), the distinctively flavored Jerusalem artichoke is a knobbly tuber with thin, pale-brown skin and creamy-white flesh. It is a native of North America and was introduced to Europe in the early 17th century.

When cooked, Jerusalem artichokes have a soft, creamy texture, not unlike that of potatoes. With their slightly sweet and nutty flavor, they make a particularly good accompaniment to all kinds of rich meat, poultry, and game dishes.

When choosing Jerusalem artichokes, look for firm, smooth, evenly sized specimens. The more knobbly the artichokes, the more waste there will be when peeling them. To prepare, scrub well, then trim off any dark or woody bits and peel thinly. As soon as they have been cut, drop them right into water to which a squeeze of lemon juice has been added. This will prevent the flesh from discoloring when exposed to the air.

Jerusalem artichokes can be boiled like potatoes, then mashed, pureed, or made into soup. They are also good tossed in a creamy sauce and baked in a gratin, or roasted in olive oil until crisp and golden. When sliced wafer-thin and deep-fried, they make delicious crunchy crisps for snacking on or scooping up a creamy dip.

stoved artichokes

In a variation on the classic Scottish dish, stovies, Jerusalem artichokes are delicious steamed with a little fried garlic and stock in a covered pan. Peel about 2¼ pounds of artichokes, then cut them into chunks. Heat 2 tablespoons of olive oil in a large pot and gently fry a finely chopped clove of garlic for about 1–2 minutes, until soft. Toss in the artichokes, stirring to coat, then add about 2 tablespoons of vegetable stock, a pinch of salt, and plenty of freshly ground black pepper. Cover tightly and cook gently for about 10 minutes, stirring occasionally, until tender. Check the seasoning and serve.

NOTES

Warm Jerusalem artichoke salad

Piping hot, crisp, and golden, Jerusalem artichokes are delicious tossed with fresh salad greens—giving the substance and warmth needed in a winter salad. Serve this dish as an accompaniment or appetizer, or toss in some extra bacon and a handful of nuts and serve with crusty bread as a light lunch or supper.

SERVES 4
3 tbsp. olive oil
1¾ lb. Jerusalem artichokes, cut into chunks
salt and freshly ground black pepper
3 large handfuls salad greens, such as baby spinach, arugula, and watercress
4 strips of bacon, fried until crispy

FOR THE DRESSING
1 tsp. Dijon mustard
1 tsp. grated lemon rind
1 tbsp. white wine vinegar
pinch of sugar
3 tbsp. olive oil

Heat the oven to 400°F. Pour the oil into a roasting pan and place in the oven. Meanwhile, cook the artichokes in boiling salted water for about 10 minutes, until just tender.

Drain the artichokes and let them steam dry, then tip into the roasting pan. Toss to coat in the oil and cook in the oven for about 25 minutes, tossing from time to time, until crisp and golden.

Meanwhile, make the dressing. Blend together the mustard, lemon rind, vinegar, and sugar in a small bowl, then whisk in the olive oil and season to taste with salt and pepper.

Arrange the salad greens on four serving plates, then scatter the hot artichokes over them and crumble the bacon over the top. Drizzle with the dressing and serve immediately.

Spiced Jerusalem artichokes

SERVES 4
2 tbsp. olive oil
1 onion, cut in half and thinly sliced
2 cloves garlic, crushed
1 tsp. ground cumin
1 tsp. ground coriander seed
large pinch of dried red pepper flakes
1 lb. Jerusalem artichokes, cut into large pieces
salt
¼ cup water
juice of ¼ lemon

Heat the oil in a large pot. Add the onion and garlic and fry gently for about 5 minutes, until soft. Stir in the ground cumin, ground coriander seed, and red pepper flakes and cook for about 30 seconds.

Toss in the Jerusalem artichokes, season to taste with salt, and pour in the water. Stir to combine well, bring to a gentle simmer, cover the pot, and cook over a low heat for about 20 minutes until the artichokes are tender.

Check the seasoning and add more salt if necessary, then squeeze the lemon juice over it, and serve.

parsnips and other roots

The cold winter months are the time really to make the most of root vegetables, which, thankfully, are in plentiful supply then and can be enjoyed in a wealth of hearty warming dishes. Parsnips, turnips, rutabagas, salsifies, and even kohlrabi grace the produce shelves alongside staples such as potatoes and carrots. They all have their own delicious and distinctive flavor and texture and can be cooked together or separately.

Turnips and rutabagas (also called "swedes") are similarly robust vegetables and can often be substituted for each other in recipes. They are both wonderful cut up in chunky soups and stews, as well as mashed or roasted. Parsnips have an almost honeyed flavor and go particularly well with warm spices. When they are roasted, their natural sugars caramelize, giving a wonderfully crisp, golden, and sticky result.

When choosing root vegetables, look for firm specimens. Buy them still covered in earth if possible, as their flavor will be far better. Avoid any with dark or soft patches. Most roots keep well, but should be stored in a cool dark place to prevent them from sprouting.

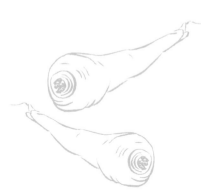

root vegetable crisps (opposite)

Crisps made from wafer-thin slices of root vegetables are easy to prepare, and are great served with drinks. Serve on their own or with a little dish of garlic mayonnaise for dipping. You can use any root vegetable you like. Try a mix of parsnips and potatoes, for example. Or, for a contrasting dash of color, add a few carrots and perhaps some beets. First prepare the vegetables: trim and peel, then use a mandoline or vegetable peeler (or a sharp knife) to slice them into thin shavings. Rinse well, then pat dry on paper towels. Fill a pan about one-third full with sunflower oil and heat to 375°F. Working in batches, deep-fry the vegetables for about 1 minute until crisp and golden. Lift out of the oil using a slotted spoon, and drain on a wire rack covered with several layers of paper towel. Sprinkle with salt and serve immediately.

Curried parsnip soup

SERVES 4
2 tbsp. olive oil
1 onion, chopped
2 cloves garlic, finely chopped
1-inch piece fresh ginger,
peeled and grated
5 large parsnips, chopped
¼ tsp. dried red pepper flakes
1 tsp. ground cumin
1 tsp. ground coriander seed
¼ tsp. turmeric
5 cups vegetable stock
juice of ½ lemon
plain yogurt and nan bread,
for serving

Heat the oil in a large pot, then add the onion, garlic, and ginger and fry gently for about 5 minutes, until the onion is tender.

Stir in the parsnips, red pepper flakes, cumin, coriander seed, and turmeric, then pour in the stock and bring to a boil. Reduce the heat, cover, and let simmer for about 15 minutes, until the parsnips are tender.

Tip into a blender or food processor and blend until smooth. Return to the pot and stir in lemon juice to taste. Ladle into bowls, drizzle with yogurt, and serve with wedges of warm nan bread.

Sautéed salsify in butter with herbs

Serve these crisp golden roots as a side dish, or scatter them over a simple salad of winter salad greens tossed with broiled scallions, crispy bacon, and a drizzle of vinaigrette.

SERVES 4
1¼ lb. salsifies
salt and freshly ground black pepper
2 tbsp. butter
grated rind of 1 lemon
large handful of fresh flat-leaf
parsley, roughly chopped

Peel the salsifies and cut into thick 2-inch-long sticks, placing them in water mixed with a splash of lemon juice to prevent them discoloring, as you go. Bring a pot of salted water to a boil, add the salsify, and cook for about 15 minutes until tender, then drain well and let them steam dry.

In a frying pan, melt the butter until sizzling, then add the cooked salsify and sauté for about 5 minutes until crisp and golden. Sprinkle the lemon rind and parsley over it, season to taste with black pepper, and serve immediately.

NOTES

Salsify mash

This light and tangy version of classic mash is delicious served with meat and game. The olive oil and lemon juice balance the subtle flavor of the salsifies perfectly.

SERVES 4
1¼ lb. salsifies
2 tbsp. olive oil
juice of ½ lemon
salt and freshly ground black pepper

Peel the salsifies and cut into chunks, placing them in water to which a splash of lemon juice has been added to stop them discoloring, as you go. Bring a pot of lightly salted water to a boil. Toss in the salsify chunks and cook for about 15 minutes until tender, then drain well.

Mash the salsifies until smooth, stir in the olive oil and lemon juice to taste, and season well with black pepper. Serve.

Kohlrabi stewed with tomatoes and spices

Kohlrabi makes a wonderfully rich and hearty stew. During cooking it becomes deliciously sweet and tender, blending well with the juicy tomatoes, flavorsome garlic, and warm spices.

SERVES 4
2 tbsp. olive oil
2 cloves garlic, finely chopped
1 tsp. ground cumin
¼ tsp. dried red pepper flakes
5 kohlrabi, quartered
14½-oz. can chopped tomatoes
½ tsp. turmeric
salt and freshly ground black pepper

Heat the oil in a large pan. Add the garlic and fry gently for about 2 minutes, then stir in the cumin and red pepper flakes and fry for another 30 seconds.

Stir in the kohlrabi, followed by the tomatoes and turmeric. Season to taste with salt and pepper and bring to a boil. Reduce the heat, cover, and let it simmer for about 30 minutes until the kohlrabi is tender. Serve.

cranberries

Related to bilberries and blueberries, bright-red oval cranberries are harder and bigger and have a much sharper flavor. They come into season in late autumn and last right through the winter. Always cooked, they are often made into a piquant sauce that is traditionally served with turkey at Christmas and Thanksgiving. The berries are also good for turning into preserves and can be added to innumerable desserts. Because their flavor is naturally sharp, they are often best combined with other fruits. They make, for example, a good addition to apple crumble or pie and are great in cakes and muffins or added to sweetened tea-breads. Their natural astringency adds interest to all these dishes, offsetting the sweetness of other ingredients.

The hard, waxy berries contain a natural preservative, benzoic acid, which means they keep better than most berries. When buying, look for firm, shiny berries, avoiding any that are soft or shriveled. If adding sugar to cranberries in a recipe, such as a sauce, do so after the berries have cooked a little and "popped," otherwise they will not soften.

Cranberry and apple muffins *(opposite)*

MAKES 12
2¾ cups self-rising flour
½ cup sugar
1 tsp. ground cinnamon
½ cup milk
2 large eggs, beaten
½ cup (1 stick) butter, melted
1 eating apple, peeled, cored and finely chopped
large handful of fresh cranberries

Heat the oven to 400°F. Line a 12-cup muffin pan with paper muffin cups.

Sift the flour, sugar, and cinnamon into a large bowl and make a well in the center. In a large measuring cup, combine the milk, beaten eggs, melted butter, and chopped apple. Pour into the well in the flour mixture and mix briefly until just combined.

Drop a spoonful of the mixture into the bottom of each muffin cup, top each with a few cranberries, then spoon the remaining mixture on top and sprinkle a few more cranberries on top.

Bake in the oven for about 25 minutes until risen and golden. Remove the muffins from the pan and leave on a wire rack to cool slightly before serving.

Winter

NOTES

chestnuts

Chestnuts are traditionally given a special place at the Christmas table. These shiny brown nuts are delicious boiled or roasted—always split the hard skin first to stop them exploding while cooking—and eaten on their own. They are also good pureed and served as a side dish or mixed into stuffings. Tossed with freshly cooked Brussels sprouts, a pat of butter, and freshly ground black pepper, they make one of the best vegetable dishes on the winter menu.

In southern Europe, they have a long culinary history, being used in breads, cakes, and sweetmeats and to make a type of flour. Chestnuts have a natural affinity with chocolate and you will find many recipes for rich chocolate desserts, ice creams, and cakes that include them.

Most recipes for chestnuts call for them to be cooked and peeled, and although this is simple to do, you can buy ready-prepared chestnuts in cans or vacuum packs. These also have the advantage of being available at any time of the year. Canned chestnut puree is available, too.

Chestnut and hazelnut roast

SERVES 6-8
¾ cup hazelnuts
2 tbsp. olive oil
1 onion, finely chopped
2 cloves garlic, finely chopped
8 oz. mushrooms, finely chopped
(about 2-2½ cups)
salt and freshly ground black pepper
8 oz. chestnuts, cooked, peeled and finely chopped
1¾ cups fresh white bread crumbs
pinch of dried thyme
¼ cup vegetable stock
juice of ½ lemon

Heat the oven to 400°F. Grease a 9 x 5 x 3-inch loaf pan and line the bottom with parchment paper.

Put the hazelnuts in a food processor and run it briefly to chop finely, but avoid grinding to a smooth powder. Set aside.

Heat the oil in a large pan, add the onion and garlic, and gently fry for about 5 minutes, until tender. Add the mushrooms, sprinkle with a little salt, and cook gently for about 10 minutes, until the mushrooms are tender and most of the liquid has evaporated. They should be moist, but not wet.

Remove the pan from the heat and stir in the hazelnuts, chestnuts, bread crumbs, thyme, stock, and lemon juice, and season with salt and pepper. Press the mixture into the loaf pan and bake in the oven for about 30 minutes, until golden. Let the roast stand for about 5 minutes, then very carefully invert it onto a board or serving platter, cut into slices, and serve.

NOTES

what's in season when

Seasonality is subject to change and is really something of a moveable feast. The chart opposite will give you an indication of when most fruits and vegetables are likely to come into season and be at their best. But in areas with a warmer-than-average climate compared to the rest of the country, many may be ready to harvest a month or so earlier in the year than is stated.

Also, weather conditions may vary from year to year, causing crops to develop earlier or later than expected. Remember, too, that cooler-than-average temperatures may, in fact, benefit some crops, by giving them the time to grow more slowly and so develop their flavors to their maximum potential. Others, however, will be hampered in their development without long days of constant sunshine to help them to ripen and sweeten and so achieve their full glory.

A large number of fruits and vegetables is available across several seasons—perhaps arriving on the shelves at the end of winter and lasting right through until the early part of the summer—while others are around only for a couple of months or even weeks. Still more, such as apples, pears, and many root vegetables, may be available from cold-storage, tasting just as fresh and delicious as they ever were, long after their peak growing season is over.

Because of the delightful flexibility of nature when it comes to growing seasons, this book should be used only as a guide for what to look out for in the stores and supermarkets as the year progresses. By far the best way of always making sure that you obtain seasonal produce at its very best is to get to know your suppliers—ask them what is likely to be available when, what is grown locally, and what is at its freshest and highest quality every time you visit them. This might not be so practical in a supermarket, whose produce may have traveled 3,000 miles but in the summer, if you have a roadside vegetable stand nearby, they should be able to answer your questions. Or you could try growing some produce in your own yard. The taste of ingredients cooked within hours of picking is truly sensational and can open up a whole new world of surprising depths and subtleties of flavor.

INGREDIENT	SPRING	SUMMER	AUTUMN	WINTER
apples	cold store	cold store	in season	cold store
apricots		in season		
artichokes, globe	in season	in season	in season	
artichokes, Jerusalem				in season
arugula	in season	in season	in season	in season
Asian greens	in season		in season	in season
asparagus	in season			
avocados	in season	in season	in season	in season
basil		in season		
beans		in season	in season	
beets		in season	in season	cold store
Belgian endive	in season		in season	in season
bell peppers		in season	in season	
blackberries			in season	
black currants		in season		
blueberries		in season		
broccoli, calabrese		in season	in season	
broccoli romanesco		in season	in season	
Brussels sprouts			in season	in season
cabbages	in season	in season	in season	in season
carrots	in season	in season	in season	cold store
cauliflowers	in season	in season	in season	in season
celeriac (celery root)			in season	in season
celery			in season	
cherries		in season		
chestnuts			in season	in season
chicory, curly	in season	in season	in season	in season
chives	in season	in season		
cilantro (coriander leaves)	in season	in season		
corn		in season	in season	
crab apples			in season	
cranberries			in season	in season
cucumbers		in season	in season	

INGREDIENT	SPRING	SUMMER	AUTUMN	WINTER
dandelion leaves	in season	in season		
dill	in season	in season		
eggplants		in season	in season	
elderberries			in season	
elderflowers		in season		
fennel			in season	
figs			in season	
game			in season	
garlic	in season	in season	cold store	cold store
garlic, wild	in season			
gooseberries		in season		
grapes			in season	
kale				in season
kohlrabi		in season	in season	in season
lamb	in season	in season	in season	in season
leeks	in season		in season	in season
lettuces	in season	in season		
marjoram	in season	in season		
medlars			in season	
melons		in season	in season	
mint	in season	in season	in season	
morels	in season			
mushrooms			in season	
nettles	in season			
okra		in season		
onions	cold store	cold store	in season	cold store
oregano	in season	in season		
parsley	in season	in season	in season	
parsnips			in season	in season
peaches		in season	in season	
pears	cold store		in season	cold store
peas		in season		
plums			in season	

INGREDIENT	SPRING	SUMMER	AUTUMN	WINTER
pomegranates			in season	
potatoes	cold store	cold store	in season	in season
potatoes, new	in season			
pumpkins			in season	
quinces			in season	
raspberries		in season		
red currants		in season		
rhubarb	in season			in season
rose hips			in season	
rosemary		in season	in season	
rutabaga			in season	in season
sage	in season	in season	in season	in season
salsifies			in season	in season
scallions (green onions)	in season	in season	in season	in season
shallots		in season	in season	
sloes			in season	
sorrel	in season	in season		
spinach	in season	in season	in season	in season
spring greens	in season			
squashes, summer		in season	in season	
squashes, winter			in season	in season
strawberries		in season		
sweet potatoes			in season	in season
Swiss chard	in season		in season	in season
tarragon		in season		
thyme	in season	in season	in season	
tomatoes		in season	in season	
turnips			in season	in season
watercress	in season	in season	in season	in season
white currants		in season		
zucchinis		in season	in season	

index

acknowledgments

My thanks to all the food writers, whose
work I have read and been influenced by
over the years, but in particular to Jane
Grigson, Hugh Fearnley-Whittingstall,
Paul Waddington, Xanthe Clay, and
Madhur Jaffrey. And, of course, enormous
thanks to all my friends and family for
their enthusiasm and appetites, and to
Grace Cheetham and all the team at
Duncan Baird for helping me bring this
book to fruition.

index